rubber!

JANET BLOOR · JOHN D. SINCLAIR

rubber!

fun, fashion, fetish

Thames & Hudson

contents

Who can examine, and reflect upon this property
of gum-elastic, without adoring the wisdom of the creator?

from *Gum-Elastic*, Charles Goodyear, New Haven, 1855

RUBBER

Strong and stylish, flexible and fun. It shares our most
lovable personality traits and appeals to us on a human,
emotional level.
This book stems from my lifelong fascination with rubber.
The following pages consist of passion, pure and simple –
passion for a substance that crosses all cultural lines and
affects our modern lives in ways both subtle and colossal.
From duckies and designer dresses to Dalí's melting
clocks, rubber is both a model of function and a
master of form. Step into these pages and
you'll find yourself on a virtual safari,
witnessing rubber in its wild and native habitat,
exploring its infinite uses, transformations, shapes, and disguises.
Rubber's diversity and versatility in almost any design context
yield vivid sensations and powerful images every step of
the way.
Until now, the only books available on rubber have been
scientific and historical dissertations – hardly enough to stretch
a roving imagination. This book is designed to fill that gap and,
in addition to its joy in artistry, it is meant to serve as a quick and
valuable reference guide.
Enter and enjoy: it is time to bring the world of rubber
into the spotlight.

FOREWORD

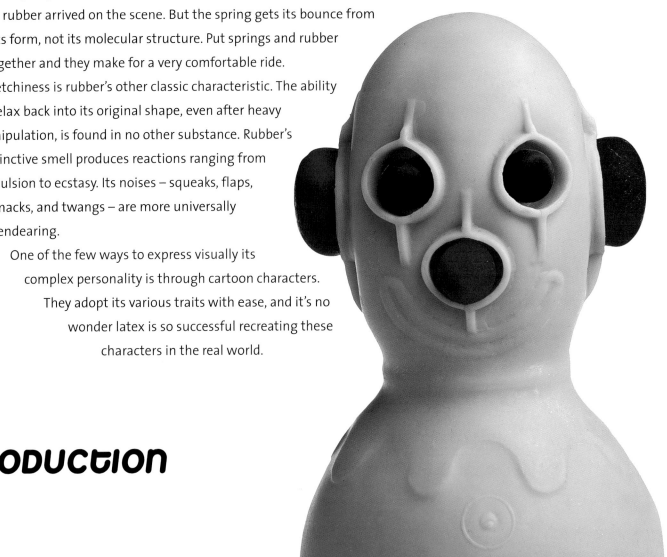

Naked, honest, malleable, willing, and strong, rubber is the stuff from which dreams are made.

What sets it apart from all other materials? Bounce, for sure. The spring came first, cushioning us faithfully – along with padding – before rubber arrived on the scene. But the spring gets its bounce from its form, not its molecular structure. Put springs and rubber together and they make for a very comfortable ride. Stretchiness is rubber's other classic characteristic. The ability to relax back into its original shape, even after heavy manipulation, is found in no other substance. Rubber's distinctive smell produces reactions ranging from repulsion to ecstasy. Its noises – squeaks, flaps, smacks, and twangs – are more universally endearing.

One of the few ways to express visually its complex personality is through cartoon characters. They adopt its various traits with ease, and it's no wonder latex is so successful recreating these characters in the real world.

INTRODUCTION

The hardest thing to get across in
a book is the tactile nature of rubber – its
supple capacity to change and deform constantly
during use. Rubber must be touched to be fully
appreciated. Rubber fetishists know this – to them it's the
ultimate sensual experience. Most people, however, find it strange to
consider rubber in its pure state, and prefer to think of its qualities
channeled into objects they can relate to. This book celebrates these objects, many
of which don't have designers or inventors on hand to take credit for their existence.
Rubber is often taken for granted, but when it begs for attention, as we shall see, it
generally gets it.
Walk through a museum and you'll see plenty of mankind's greatest achievements, but
you won't see many exhibits devoted to rubber. This snub should not be seen as a bad
thing – on the contrary, it's a backhanded tribute to rubber's universal acceptance
and common importance. Rubber camouflages itself into our lives with such
expertise that we hardly give it a thought.
Consider the wide and disparate ways this material's qualities have been
utilized. We see the basic tasks it performs – tires, wires, handles of
pliers – but we overlook the vital part it plays in many other
spheres of our lives. Its flexibility and resistance
have paved the way for a multitude

of advances in design, technology, and lifestyle. Rubber grips the road, but it also grips the imagination.

For those intrigued by the bigger mysteries of life, there is a profound zen-like quality inherent to rubber. In many of its forms it reveals its yin and yang; its negative spaces function as an integral part of the whole. Try the trusty plunger: in the act of collapsing into its own negative space it fulfills its reason for being, and mystical duality handily unclogs your pipes.

In its natural form, rubber is a renewable, biodegradable compound native to the rainforests of South America. Although rubber has only been known about in the West for around 200 years, the tribes and cultures of Central and South America have been aware of its properties for centuries. Both natural and synthetic rubbers have made their own special contributions over the years – there are many types of rubber, many more than are featured here – but one thing they have in common is a tendency to decay over time, one reason there are so few remaining early objects made from rubber material.

Rubber has rarely been used to fabricate lavish products and, in true utilitarian form, rubber items have traditionally been designed to literally wear away. Sophisticated, stylish, refined – these words are not usually associated with rubber. Yet in a startling moment in the 1992 French film *Indochine*, Catherine Deneuve confesses it's the smell of rubber that keeps her on the plantation. This remark from the queen of class essentially put rubber in a top hat and tails.

Rubbernecking – one of the more amusing uses the word has been plundered for – describes our cartoonish behavior in an apt way.

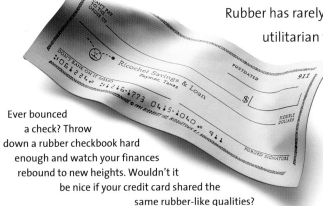

Ever bounced a check? Throw down a rubber checkbook hard enough and watch your finances rebound to new heights. Wouldn't it be nice if your credit card shared the same rubber-like qualities?

The very word rubber has taken on a risqué connotation. Make a comment like "I love rubber" during general conversation and see how many strange looks you get. Bring up rubber at a dinner party and count the eyebrows that rise, like helium balloons, up a horizon of foreheads. It is nothing new – the usual response is a blend of surprise, suspicion, fascination, prudishness, even titillation.

Society now associates the word "rubber" with condoms. And it's no wonder, we've been encouraged to use rubber as a go-between during our most intimate encounters with others. Naturally, the middle-man gets a naughty reputation. It knows our deepest secrets, it does our dirty work. But while rubber embraces this role as our sexual guardian and secret friend, this is just one role of many for the world's greatest shape-shifter.

In today's frantic world, where stress and worry have become the norm, rubber is calling out to us with a bigger, more important message:

LIGHTEN UP!

This is rubber's forte. Bouncy, stretchy, naughty, squeaky – the very words we use to describe it are lighthearted. This book is about celebrating rubber's good nature and its countless contributions to our lives, mundane and imaginative. Although it's a sad fact that many classic rubber objects are now also made in vinyl, the versatility of good old-fashioned rubber demands that we study its uses, history, structure...its very soul.

In recent years, the marketing potential for its sweet pungency has been captured by a perfume company that sells "Rubber Cult" in a bottle.

Only when you can be extremely pliable
and soft can you be extremely hard and strong

Zen Proverb

The South American Indians saw the milky drops of latex seeping from the rubber tree's bark and thought of big, white tears. They named the tree *cau-chu*, meaning "weeping wood." It was another spectacle among the countless bizarre and wonderful forms of plant and animal life to be found in the Amazon rainforests – an integral part of one of the richest ecosystems on earth. The natives of Latin America learnt to put this spectacle to use in practical ways, dipping their feet into bowls of latex, letting it dry into waterproof shoes. It also came in handy for crafting water bottles and other watertight items. But it wasn't until Europeans took the substance back with them that the modern rubber industry sprang on to the world scene.

RUBBER SOUL

The Omagua Indians of the Amazon had long called the rubber tree sap *heve*, which led to the botanical name *Hevea brasiliensis*. As the substance took root in Europe, *heve* was given new names. The French adapted *cau-chu* to *caoutchouc* when Charles Marie de la Condamine first brought it back and published his observations in 1745. Variations of the French spelling are used as the word for rubber in most European countries.

The Portuguese called rubber *seringa* after one of its more common uses – the syringe. This was then adapted to *seringueiros*, as the rubber tappers became known. As the rainforests fall victim to modern industry's slashing and burning, today's *seringueiros* fight to save the forests and their livelihoods. *Seringueiro* Chico Mendes (1944–88) helped make us aware of the ecological disasters caused by companies in search of "cheap" materials. He knew how important it was to preserve not only the birthplace of rubber, but of so many things that impact the planet and ourselves.

English chemist Joseph Priestly gave us the English word rubber in 1770, on discovering it could erase pencil marks. His discovery must have been greeted with the same enthusiasm later given to white-out or the delete button. The eraser's impact is obvious, modern software programs retain the eraser icon and method, allowing the 200-year-old technique to sweep across your computer screen in a user friendly gesture.

This natural rubber snake is an Amazonian souvenir, created by locals for the tourist trade. It captures both the essence of the Amazon River and the nature of the latex in its fluid and wiggly form.

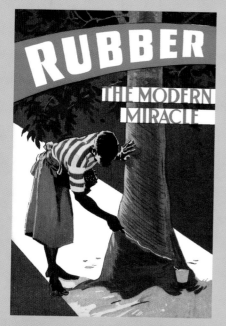

The early 20th century saw rubber companies expounding the virtues of rubber in informative booklets, generally aimed at children. Publications such as *The Romance of Rubber* give a hugely idealized image of wild rubber collecting in South America and Africa. Life was a little easier on the company plantations in the Far East but, in either case, the life of a rubber tapper was not to be envied.

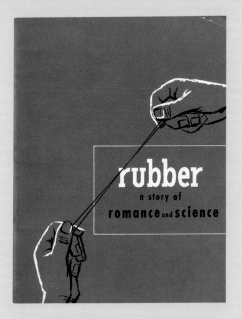

the rubber family tree

includes nearly 2,000 latex-producing relatives. Ficus trees are on the list, along with Christmas poinsettias. In fact, just about all plants that ooze milk when broken belong to the rubber family. *Hevea Brasiliensis* stands alone, however, in its capacity for commercial rubber production. Although the soul of rubber remains firmly rooted in the Amazon, its lifeblood was long ago transplanted to the Far East, where plantation rubber supplies most of the world's needs. Modern tree breeding has increased output to around five times more than in the early plantation days. One tree — mature after seven years — yields up to four gallons of latex a year, and has a productive life of between 25 and 30 years.

93.

Turpin. P.

Lambert J° sculp.

CAOUT-CHOUC.

Where is our Natural Rubber?

Rubber grows in a belt that stretches around the world, from 700 miles above the Equator to 700 miles below. In this hot, tropical area are the rubber plantations. More than 95% of all our natural rubber comes from the Far East — Malaya, Indonesia, Thailand, Ceylon and other Asian countries. The rest comes from Liberia, other African countries and Latin America.

ASIA

MALAYA

SUMATRA

BORNEO

INDONESIA

JAVA

Rubber change mats were popular items in the 1940s and 1950s. This Chiclets change mat uses one kind of rubber to advertise another.

Sapodilla, another member of the rubber family, produces Chicle gum and was the original base for chewing gum. The first flavored gum to hit the market was made from and named after the Mexican Yucatán region, and it helped trigger the modern gum industry. Many years of synthetic substitutes have made way for a return of the natural variety, which has come back with such names as Speakeasy and Glee Gum.

Putting Industry on Rubber Heels

It is difficult to imagine the automotive, marine, and aeronautical industries without rubber, its presence helps all general manufacturing processes with simple devices such as conveyors, conducting belts, insulation, gaskets, glues, and shock-absorbers. But it took many years and innumerable experiments to make rubber viable for industrial use.

INDUSTRIAL RUBBER PRODUCTS

CATALOG 52

ESTABLISHED 1919

ATLANTIC INDIA RUBBER WORKS, INC.
571 WEST POLK STREET · · CHICAGO 7, ILLINOIS
DESIGNERS   ALL TELEPHONES HARRISON 7-8290   ENGINEERS

MANUFACTURERS MOLDED AND FABRICATED INDUSTRIAL RUBBER PRODUCTS

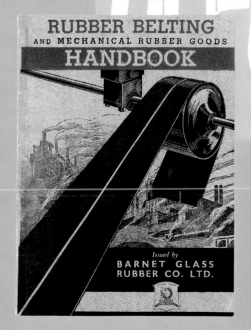

RUBBER BELTING
AND MECHANICAL RUBBER GOODS
HANDBOOK

Issued by
BARNET GLASS
RUBBER CO. LTD.

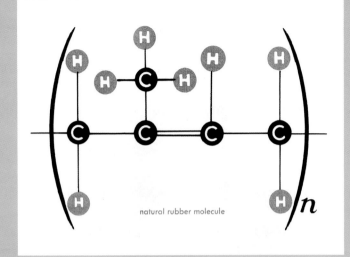

natural rubber molecule

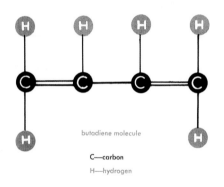

butadiene molecule

C—carbon
H—hydrogen

UNTIL THE DISCOVERY of the vulcanization process, manufacturing with natural latex proved disastrous, and for decades rubber remained nothing more than a promising novelty. The early rubber industry suffered massive losses as stocks of rubber goods melted together into useless blobs. Scientifically defined as a liquid, rubber becomes softer and more fluid as temperatures rise. Thus, a basic chemistry problem needed solving before rubber's unique qualities could be harnessed.

The natural rubber molecule is gigantic, consisting of long chains of carbon and hydrogen atoms, wiggling in all directions. Resembling an unraveled sweater, these polymers mass together in tangled groups, and are in their liquid state at temperatures above -72°C, accounting for rubber's flexibility at room temperature. Rubber's polymers can stretch out considerably as the molecular structure uncoils, displaying great elasticity. When the breaking point is reached and the polymers can stretch no more, they could technically be considered fibers – but such is their recoil strength that they spring back into their coils.

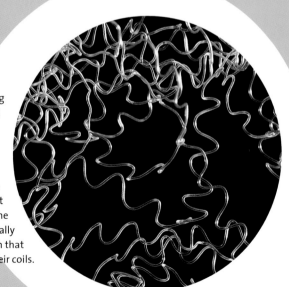

A furniture designer working with pine could switch to mahogany and reproduce a chair with the same functionality. This flexibility in design, ironically, does not extend to rubber. Since the ingredients are constantly changing states throughout processing, and even on completion, the chemists and engineers are the true designers. Working with variables such as elongation, plasticity, strength, abrasion, and resistance, rubber articles are wholly dependent on the recipe being precise if they are to function at all, and the function of the finished product always determines its chemistry.

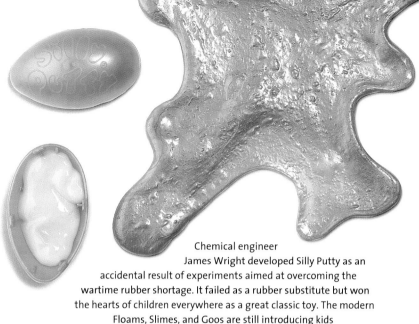

Chemical engineer James Wright developed Silly Putty as an accidental result of experiments aimed at overcoming the wartime rubber shortage. It failed as a rubber substitute but won the hearts of children everywhere as a great classic toy. The modern Floams, Slimes, and Goos are still introducing kids to the strangeness of rubber.

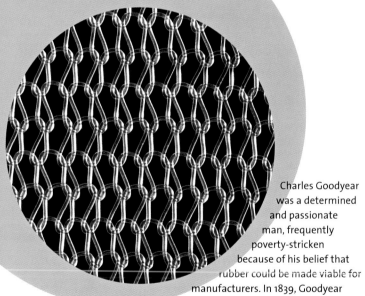

Charles Goodyear was a determined and passionate man, frequently poverty-stricken because of his belief that rubber could be made viable for manufacturers. In 1839, Goodyear finally patented the use of sulfur as a stabilizing agent. Combined with heat, sulfur causes chemical cross-linking between rubber's polymers, providing the magic method everyone was searching for. The process was named vulcanization, after Vulcan, the Roman god of fire, and it did for the rubber industry what silicon chips did for computers.

Dynamic Isolation Systems manufactures bearings that float entire buildings in earthquake zones, and natural rubber is the company's material of choice. Its qualities in such sensitive situations are superior to those of synthetics, and its range of motion is remarkable.

20

Here he is, the crowned head of rubber imagery and hero of the bath. Jolly and sexless, always smiling, the rubber duck is more widely recognized than Mickey Mouse, with none of the commercial undertones. He has no need to identify with any product; he represents a timeless way of life, an ageless philosophy. Identified with, but not limited to the baby years and the bathtub, his image is still everywhere and his smile hasn't faded. His message is clear: *fun*.

Babies are the real winners when it comes to rubber's capacity for fun. How long did some enterprising parent bounce a baby on his or her knee before inventing the baby bouncer? Translated into an adult sport, thrill-seekers put their lives on the rubber line, relying on the integrity, elongation, and tear strength of the bungee cord. Possibly based on rites of passage into adulthood by natives of the Pentecost Islands (who bravely use yam vines to break their falls), bungee jumpers trust the rubber to thrill them yet keep them safe, recalling our own fearlessness and trust when our parents threw us into the air.

RUBBER DUCKY

Exhilaration and security: we need both to live, but how often can you get both vital commodities in the same deal? It is during childhood that we begin to explore the more unusual properties of rubber, and it is here that we also find many of the classic uses. It can form itself into an infinite variety of shapes, always retaining its integrity, always ready to bounce right back. It's no wonder we use it in so many ways.

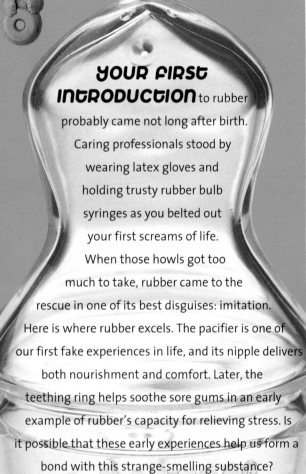

YOUR FIRST INTRODUCTION to rubber probably came not long after birth. Caring professionals stood by wearing latex gloves and holding trusty rubber bulb syringes as you belted out your first screams of life. When those howls got too much to take, rubber came to the rescue in one of its best disguises: imitation. Here is where rubber excels. The pacifier is one of our first fake experiences in life, and its nipple delivers both nourishment and comfort. Later, the teething ring helps soothe sore gums in an early example of rubber's capacity for relieving stress. Is it possible that <u>these early experiences</u> help us form a bond with this strange-smelling substance?

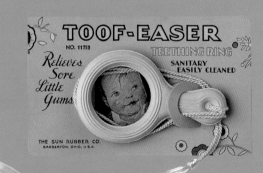

The first squeaky hollow rubber toys were
assembled in 1859 by the New York
Rubber Company. The company used
reeds to create the "squeak," thus
introducing these classic toys, which
would stand the test of time.
Nearly a century later, Rempel
of Akron, Ohio, produced a
vast array of squeaky
animal toys.

China produced the first balloons several hundred years ago. They were made of paper.

In 1783, the first rubberized silk balloon took flight. Later that year in Versailles, Louis XVI cheered on an early group of brave but baffled ballooning pioneers: a rooster, a sheep, and a duck.

The advent of foam rubber brought about the bendy toy. Forming the foam on a wire skeleton produced a soft and malleable interactive plaything. These examples include some traditional British Bendy toys from the 1960s and 1970s.

In 1785 the postal service was changed forever when France received its first airmail from England, taking two hours by balloon.

BALLOONS AND BENDY TOYS

BALLOONS AND BENDY TOYS are part of the character forming years, which bring forth a smorgasbord of rubber playthings, but the affection we reserve for balloons lasts a lifetime. Bobbing on the end of a string like a friendly ghost, they are the guest of honor at parties, playmate to the infant in the stroller, and twisty-tie to the clown. The balloon is the closest we get to catching the elusive bubble. Its fragile form clearly displays the pressure that keeps it alive. We squeeze balloons to show us their limits, reeling when they finally burst. We punch them mercilessly, or fill them to breaking point and let them rocket off on a stream of their own pent-up energy, careering madly into oblivion.

The newer Mylar impostors lack the simplicity of the latex originals, bringing negative PR to a previously unblemished product. Released Mylar balloons have been blamed for the destruction of marine life.

The Delasson family of France blew life into the first rubber balloons around 1830.

More recently, Bendys have become generic friends. The Roundheads are blank characters that can be turned into practically anything by an active imagination.

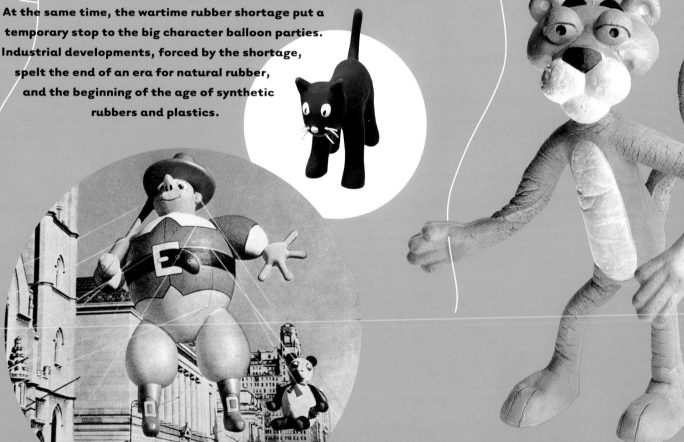

Balloons can, of course, get really big. On Thanksgiving Day, the mammoth characters floating down Broadway in New York are big enough to eat the parade-goers below. Although no longer made of pure rubber, their ancestors were. In fact, the giant Macy's character balloons were originally set free to float out of the city, but the advent of air traffic put a stop to that. No pilot was prepared for a giant Felix the Cat closing in at six o'clock. The war machine capitalized on this concept by using massive barrage balloons tethered to the ground, bobbing annoyingly and interfering with enemy aircraft.

At the same time, the wartime rubber shortage put a temporary stop to the big character balloon parties. Industrial developments, forced by the shortage, spelt the end of an era for natural rubber, and the beginning of the age of synthetic rubbers and plastics.

In angioplasty a balloon is used to open narrowed or blocked blood vessels of the heart. Balloons are good for closing things, too – sealing off a burst water main, for example.

In 1794, revolutionary France put balloons to military use, establishing the first balloon air corps. Napoleon Bonaparte staged several displays to show off the power of his corps, and the Austrians also used them for air-bombing during the upheavals of 1849. Observation balloons during the Zeppelin raids on London sparked the creation of barrage balloons.

BALL·MAKING was one of the earliest uses for rubber. Columbus introduced these balls to Queen Isabella of Spain on his return from the New World, where ball games were an integral part of the Mesoamerican culture. The Mayans and Aztecs built grand ball courts where religious and cultural games were played, requiring a heavy rubber ball and carved stone hoops. Such were the status of these balls that they were found in sacred wells, alongside the remains of sacrificed victims. Decapitation at the games was not unknown, when someone decided to make a morbid swap for the ball.

Today, ball games remain among the world's most popular forms of entertainment, spanning all social classes. As for the Mayans and Aztecs, the ball provides a vehicle for patriotism and a showcase for the magnificence of the human physical condition. It rolls with us into adulthood, allowing us outbursts of freedom from inhibition that are usually reserved for children.

Ancient civilizations learnt to use the juice of Morning Glory vines, which served as a vulcanizing agent for balls such as this Mayan example. X-rays of ancient balls reveal a winding construction, like a long rubber band, similar to the way golf balls are made. A single golf ball, for example, has a liquid center wound with about 35 yards (32 meters) of rubber thread, which stretches to about 280 yards (256 meters). The added tension provides just the right kind of bounce as you smack it over the green.

Modern basketball hoops imitate these decorative stone rings at the ball court at Chichén Itzá, Mexico.

This vintage "Tornado" bowling ball is made of hard rubber, also known as Ebonite.

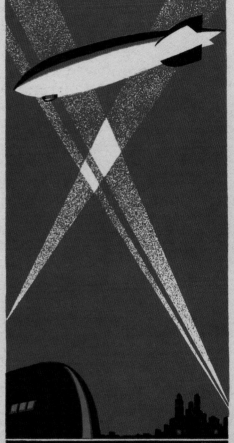

AKRON AND
U·S·S·AKRON·

WORLD'S LARGEST AIRSHIP

Complete Pictures and Story of DOCK, SHIP, AIRPORT and "Lighter-Than-Air" Center of the World.

One remnant of the great age of big balloons is the blimp, the most famous of which shares the name of Charles Goodyear — a fitting tribute to the man who spent his life making the substance viable. Another famous airship is the Zeppelin. Originally built in the 1930s, in conjunction with the Goodyear company in Akron, Ohio, the Zeppelin has recently taken to the air again. The new NTN07 Zeppelin served as a camera platform for the 2000 Olympic Games in Sydney, and as a preliminary to the larger passenger-carrying Zeppelins, which have the capacity for 86 passengers. These apparent reincarnations, retaining the old shape and framework, are waterproof, capable of landing independently, and can act as a convenient form of transport to Arctic areas. They use little energy, move without noise, and are ecologically sound. Their biggest challenge? Recovering from the negative PR that followed a little thing called the Hindenburg disaster.

The STORY OF THE AIRSHIP
by HUGH ALLEN

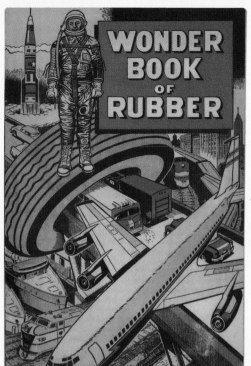

This Mexican finger puppet is made from natural rubber.

The power of rubber polymers — their inherent strength and capacity for recoiling to their twisted state — is what charges rubber with a temporary source of energy. This power can be harnessed in a number of ways. See what happens when you untie an air-filled balloon or let loose a group of tightly-wound rubber bands. Kids have found lots of ways to use this pent up energy, and popular science magazines and comic books have long encouraged such discoveries.

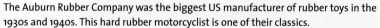

The Auburn Rubber Company was the biggest US manufacturer of rubber toys in the 1930s and 1940s. This hard rubber motorcyclist is one of their classics.

Monkey bracelet by Pylones.

Originally introduced by Ken Hakuta in the 1980s, octopus-like Wacky Wall Walkers were made from sticky rubber and walked down windows. This bug uses the same concept: its weight balanced against the stickiness of its feet creates a novelty that walks down smooth surfaces.

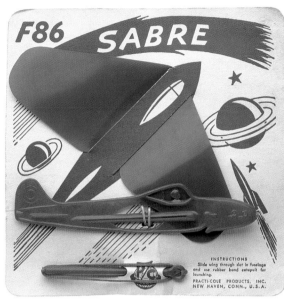

F86 SABRE

Instant retraction catapults this classic glider into the air. It was among many toys from the 1960s that were powered by rubber bands. Boat propellers and car axles captured this power by turning the bands into taut, twisty batteries.

INSTRUCTIONS
Slide wing through slot in fuselage and use rubber band catapult for launching.

PRACTI-COLE PRODUCTS, INC.
NEW HAVEN, CONN., U.S.A.

HAVE FUN MAKING THESE INTERESTING TOYS THAT ARE OPERATED BY RUBBER

1 RUBBER-BAND SWING

THE swing and figures, which are scrollsawed from plywood or hard-pressed board as shown in the cross-hatched pattern, are attached to one end of a length of clock spring which should not be stiff. The other end of the spring is inserted and bradded in a slot cut in a wooden crosspiece. This is pivoted between the uprights of a sheet-metal frame, the ends of which are bent and bolted to a wooden base. To motivate the swing a length of stiff wire is used as a connecting rod. This is stapled to the crosspiece and joins the latter to a crank that rocks the swing as it is rotated by a rubber band, which is wound tightly by a similar crank supported by a bracket at one end of the base. A leather strip slotted near one end is tacked to the crank base and slipped over the crank to hold it as the rubber band unwinds and rotates the crank arm.

2 TOY TORPEDO WITH RUBBER-BAND MOTOR POWER

WHEN launched with its propeller spinning, the torpedo performs in a realistic manner. A screw eye serves as a bearing for the propeller, and two small screw hooks take the rubber band, one being driven into the end of the propeller shaft, the other near the front of the torpedo.

5 SPOOLS AND PROPELLER TOY FOR YOUNGSTERS

EASY to make. All you need is a tin propeller, a couple of spools and a length of wire, which is bent as indicated to provide axles for the spools. The propeller is attached to the upper spool and both are bolted together by rubber band.

3 POWERFUL NEW RUBBER BAND MOTOR

SUITABLE for driving model boats, toy cars, etc. The parts needed are two small drums, two shafts and a couple of gears having about a three-to-one ratio. A crank may be soldered to the upper shaft, or the end of the shaft bent to form a crank. When assembling the motor, wind a long rubber band loosely on the upper drum and attach band to the lower drum. As the lower drum...

4 RUBBER-BAND TOY SHOOTS ARROW

EASILY produced in quantities, this toy suggests spare-time profits. Cutting eight at a time, you can turn out a large number an hour on the average band saw. White pine is used, and a ⅜ in. piece 11 in. long is sawed to the shape shown and drilled, after which it is ripped into four ¾16 in. strips on the band saw. Then the 3/16 in. strips are stacked, the slots for the rubber band made and the stock cut in half. The arrows, which are also 11 in. long, can be sawed out a number at a time by stacking several thicknesses of the stock, and it's merely a matter of seconds to tip them with inch lengths of rubber tubing.

GOODRICH

...OF POPULAR MECHANICS MAGAZINE

This novelty car uses balloon power to propel it forward, a method also used for toy helicopters. A whistle is sometimes incorporated for added effect.

For heavenly form—always choose foundations made with Lastex ... THE MIRACLE YARN THAT MAKES THINGS FIT

UNITED STATES RUBBER COMPANY · Rockefeller Center · New York

SECOND SKINS

The teenage spirit is unquenchable, and puberty brings with it new curves, and
a burning urge to display our new individuality to the world. The fads that blossom
with each generation charge the cultural air with style and energy, shaping the
fashions of the day.

Preserving the energy of youthfulness has historically been a driving force behind the
development of women's clothing, although it wasn't always comfortable to look and feel
young. A youthful figure was dearly paid for through agonizing application of metal, bones,
lacing, and brute force. Medieval torture chambers didn't fade with the Renaissance, they
just moved upstairs into ladies' bedchambers. But experimentation with rubber in clothing
marked a new era, emphasizing comfort and control.

The first European rubber factory was founded in France in 1803, for the production of ladies'
elastic garters. While some critics gave this upstart material the cold shoulder, enterprising
dressmakers quickly saw its value and began incorporating it into a variety of garments. As
this excerpt from *Journal des Dames et des Modes* of 1811 reports: "Of all the new inventions,
perhaps the most popular and most talked about is that of elastic braces. The 'old young'
disguise the size of their stomach with an elastic belt; the faded coquettes support their fallen
allurements with an elastic corset. The stockings of the *incroyable* are held up with elastic
garters, the elbow gloves of a pretty woman are attached by an elastic bracelet. It is as if a
clever artist is playing with dolls that only move with springs."

By the 1920s, the liberation of women was making itself seen not only in their outfits, but in their underpinnings as well. Elastic found its way into corsets, liberating small areas with stretch, and it has since become the reigning champion of flexibility in the fashion world. Designers began replacing traditional whalebone corset girders with "bones" made from flattened steel springs, which, in combination with elastic, spawned a revolution in comfort for undergarments. Standard elastic is comprised of latex rubber threads, woven with cotton to make a continuous strip that can be stitched into a garment. The quality and type of elastic depends on the thickness of its rubber filaments, and eventually fibers fine enough to weave into cloth were developed.

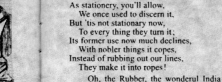

This popular song from the 1860s [far left] hints at a possible inspiration for the origin of the whoopee cushion. When women wore ducktail-style dresses, the Schrader Company prided itself on the excellent quality of the valves it created for inflatable bustles, claiming the valves would never "betray a lady in a social gathering with a hiss of failure."

No other Garment so Distinctively Different!

Support

Other Garments

Spirella

SPIRELLA is shaped below the waist to harmonize with the curves of the figure. It fits under and supports the abdomen, and is snug over the hips and back. There is no constriction at the waist. No downward pressure over the abdomen. No crowding or binding to interfere with functions of the vital organs or to retard circulation. Just a gentle support which aids nature.

The Spirella Stay

THE Spirella Stay is used exclusively in Spirella Garments. It bends freely backward and forward and sidewise. It follows readily every movement of the body. It will not take a permanent bend or push through the material and it is guaranteed not to break or rust. The flexible Spirella Stay not only permits full muscular play, but insures a shape retaining garment.

For All Types

SPIRELLA Supporting Garments are designed for the distinct individual types,—slender, medium and stout. They are made for women of varying body lengths from the shortest to the longest waisted. Such conditions as excessive flesh, over the thighs, the lower back and over the abdomen, are specifically cared for. Consequently every Spirella wearer obtains a garment to meet her individual needs.

Expert Corsetiere Service

A SPIRELLA Corsetiere comes to your home, takes your measurements and delivers to you the garment which best insures satisfaction. You are taught how to adjust and wear your Spirella to secure its full benefits. This individual attention and advice in regard to the care of your figure is a different and better service than can be found anywhere else.

Beautiful Material in the Spirit of Today

YOU can select your material from a large variety of the newest Batistes and Broches. All have passed rigid tests for quality and strength. Spirella Garments will stand repeated launderings and retain their attractive appearance and shapeliness so long, they are a real economy.

Spirella supplies its clients exclusively through Corsetieres.

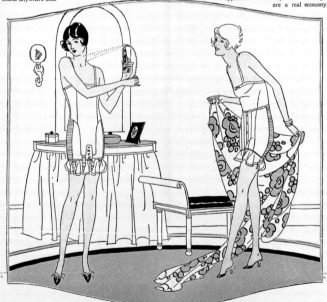

Girdles, Corsets, Brassieres, Brassiere-Girdles, Belts, Lingerie and Hosiery.

Home Service Exclusively

Spirella is Different

The modern answer to the whalebone corset incorporates flattened steel springs. The Spirella corset bone, in combination with elastic, is still used to produce a perfect balance of control and flexibility.

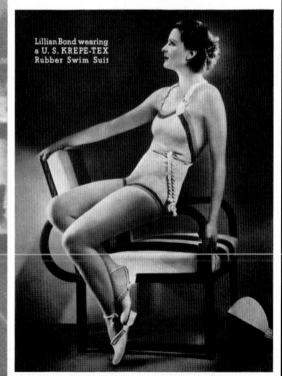

Fluent Freedom and Figure Control in gay new all-rubber swim suits!

Lillian Bond wearing a U. S. KREPE-TEX Rubber Swim Suit

Latex thread helped create the modern swimwear industry. Introduced by the United States Rubber Company in the 1930s, swimmers previously had to cope with materials that grew heavy and unwieldy when wet.

Rubber can also be used to bond together stretch fabrics, maintaining the smooth and stretchy surface of the garment. The lingerie by Michael Southgate [left] is a seamless garment that uses silicone rubber for bonding seams, and also as the stretch edge for finishing and joining different stretch fabrics.

Photo: Mark Weiss

SYNTHETIC RUBBER fibers, developed after

World War Two, went on to add even greater strength and elongation than the early latex versions, culminating in a range of fibers we have come to know as spandex. Named as an anagram of "expands," spandex is a generic name for very stretchy thread, although it has come to be known as a specific type of fabric. Initially developed by DuPont, the company's own brand of spandex thread, called Lycra, hit the market in 1959. Since then the word "Lycra" has become synonymous with "stretch" in clothing. It has revolutionized garment construction to the extent that traditional tailors are being ousted by fabrics that make their own alterations. Specialized fitting skills aren't as vital when you're dealing with material that has built-in movement. Some conservative men's suiting fabrics now incorporate up to 10-percent Lycra, allowing for a better fit straight off the rack. Exercise-, swim-, and sportswear of all types incorporate healthy portions of spandex – essential for flexibility on the ground or in the water.

The Sharkskin swimsuit by Speedo uses spandex thread knitted into a sharkskin type texture, which allows greater speed in the water.

From the catalogue of Material Connexion®, New York, this close-up of spandex fabric and silicone rubber shows a highly textured effect. The silicone is applied while the spandex fabric is stretched out, fixing the fibers in their extended state. When the fabric is relaxed, the areas treated with silicone pop up, creating texture.

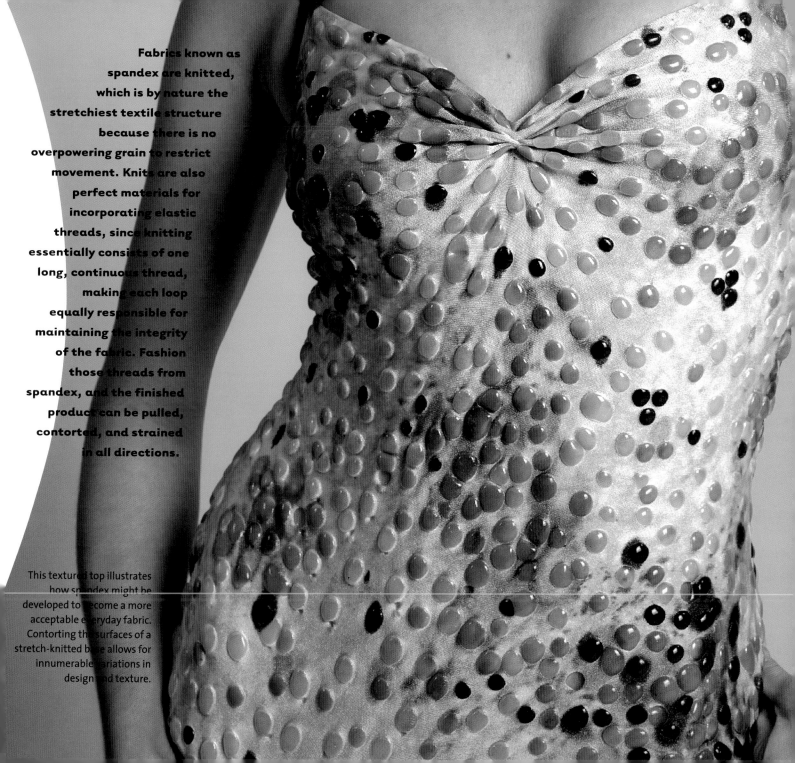

Fabrics known as spandex are knitted, which is by nature the stretchiest textile structure because there is no overpowering grain to restrict movement. Knits are also perfect materials for incorporating elastic threads, since knitting essentially consists of one long, continuous thread, making each loop equally responsible for maintaining the integrity of the fabric. Fashion those threads from spandex, and the finished product can be pulled, contorted, and strained in all directions.

This textured top illustrates how spandex might be developed to become a more acceptable everyday fabric. Contorting the surfaces of a stretch-knitted base allows for innumerable variations in design and texture.

This Victorian necklace is made from gutta-percha, a natural plastic chemically similar to rubber, originally from the Isonandra tree from Malaya. Initially used as an electrical insulator for transatlantic cables, gutta-percha eventually became more popular for golf-ball covers. Both gutta-percha and hard rubber, like this snake bracelet [left], were popular replacements for jet jewelry in the 19th century.

Watch by Armani.

Photo: Sue Broadwell

Unique Green and Black Swirl fountain pen made from hard rubber, by custom pen maker David Broadwell.

The German jeweler Bunz uses silicone rubber in combination with gold, diamonds, and other precious metals.

Photo: Jürgen Liedtke

This decorative corset by William Ivey Long is embellished with jewels and metals embedded in silicone rubber. Commissioned by Neiman Marcus for its May, 2003 catalogue cover, this butterfly costume relies totally on rubber for its fabric treatments.

INDIA·RUBBER MASKS

were first introduced in 1846 to administer ether and chloroform. Later widely used for gas masks, the more popular modern uses are for water sports. These early Welco Olympic swimming goggles by the Welsh Manufacturing Co. [above] now seem almost cartoonish when compared to the futuristic silicone scuba goggles by Dacor [below]. The malleable rubber earplugs form a perfect watertight fit, and neoprene, one of the first synthetics, is a mainstay of scuba attire.

Rubber beach buckets and spades, like this one by the Apex Tire and Rubber Co., were beach essentials for kids in the 1940s and 1950s.

Over the past 20 years, the predominance of sneakers as everyday footwear has propelled shoe technology into the space age. The standard plimsolls, although still around, have morphed into alien spaceships. Casual footwear has become high fashion on the street, marking social and financial status and sparking designer label wars.

What became a full-body fetish for many started off innocently enough — as swimming caps. A. N. Spanel founded the International Latex Company in 1932 and introduced his first "Playtex caps." The early models were relatively simple, molded and embossed with shells and sea horses, but they later blossomed into 3-D water lilies and other decorative wonders, reaching a pinnacle of embellishment by the late 1950s and 1960s. The company was eventually renamed Playtex, and the many products Spanel invented during his lifetime — approximately 2,000 — led the field with innovations for mainstream latex use.

SWIM CAPS AS ONLY *Playtex* WOULD <u>DARE</u> CREATE THEM

Perfect for running in water, the Nike Kukini sneaker is not only lightweight but crafted from a mesh, creating a sieve that lets water flow in and out freely.

rubber shoes were one of the earliest uses for the malleable new material. Rubbers first entered the US in 1820, causing a sensation because they were waterproof. Their novelty and practicality assured the material a bright future in the footwear industry. Initially crafted by hand, rubbers were seamed and joined carefully before vulcanization molded all the parts together. In the world of shoes, no other material offers the grip and friction that rubber provides. Leather soles may still be popular, but they are no match for rubber's natural cushioning and resistance.

Wellington boots were derived from a style of close-fitting boot developed by the first Duke of Wellington. Originally made from leather, they are now synonymous with rubber.

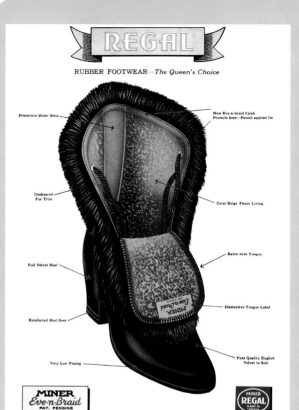

REGAL

RUBBER FOOTWEAR—The Queen's Choice

- Protective Slider Strip
- Unsheared Fur Trim
- Full Velvet Heel
- Reinforced Heel Seat
- Very Low Foxing
- New Eve-n-braid finish Protects hose—Patent applied for
- Coral Beige Fleece Lining
- Extra wide Tongue
- Distinctive Tongue Label
- First Quality English Velvet to Sole

MINER Eve-n-Braid PAT. PENDING

Tongue Label used for REGAL BRAND Overshoes

◄ 19 ►

MINER REGAL MADE IN CANADA

See this Mark of Quality on the Sole

VETO (Foothold).
(Trade-Marked and Patented.)

Men's and Women's.

Women's Medium Opera and Needle Toe.

The Veto is for use in the spring, summer, and fall, and gives just enough protection to insure dryness.

BOSTON RUBBER SHOE CO. BOSTON U.S.A. TRADE MARK

Owing to the continued increase in the use of Pointed Toe Leather Shoes, we have added largely to our styles of Pointed Toe Rubbers, a list of which may be found by referring to pages 11 and 12.

These cuts illustrate two of our most popular Needle Toe specialties.

WOMEN'S LINDEN.

MEN'S BERWICK.

A BOX OF CANDEE'S

In 1875, Charles Goodyear Junior made his name by developing a method of attaching shoe soles to uppers using a curved needle machine, a method that is still popular today.

Humphrey O'Sullivan, a printer suffering from sore feet, nailed pieces of his rubber floormat to his shoes in a frustrated attempt to stop it being stolen. In 1899 he patented his rubber heel, and the rest is history.

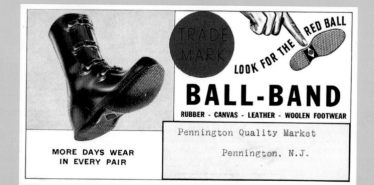

Baroness . . . slim fitting elasticized Jacquard fabric boot with umbrella self-print. Gold, silver, or black.

Caprice . . . made with all-Nylon fabric and gayly lined with a Harlequin print. Button and loop closure. Black only.

Rain-Steps . . . lightweight water-repellent, breathable fabric. Button, loop closure. Flat sole or heel. Blond, black.

Fash-n-Fit . . . elasticized fabric boot that slips on and fits like a glove—even over spike heels. Black or brown.

Kedettes
MADE IN CANADA BY
DOMINION
RUBBER COMPANY LIMITED

The display cards illustrated above are given free to Merchants handling
MINER "REGAL" RUBBER FOOTWEAR

These attractive display cards and posters are given free to Merchants handling Miner heavy rubber footwear

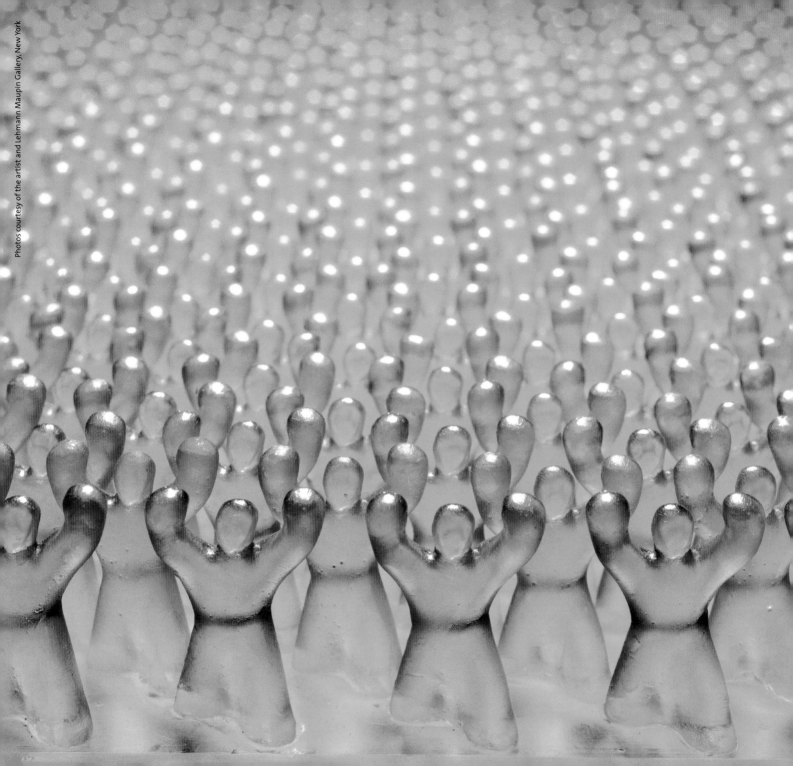

It is in mundane applications such as the ever popular "Welcome Mat," that rubber truly excels, and a random tour through any home can reveal a virtual museum of rubber treasures and modern design masterpieces.

Rubber is the top performer in the seals and gaskets business, and can really take the pressure when there is a vacuum that needs filling. It is used around the tops of jars and bottles of every kind to keep in the freshness. Even supermarket drinks bottles use a hint of a rubber seal. It works as caulking around windows to keep the cold out. Planes, trains, and automobiles all use the stuff as an essential component for operating smoothly.

Korean artist Do Ho Suh uses multitudes of welcoming people [close-up opposite] to magnify the traditional message of the doormat with his piece "Welcome Mat."

Not only the mediator in high-pressure situations, rubber also acts as the go-between in plenty of more down-to-earth ways. Being non-slip, insulating, and waterproof, it's invaluable in every room in the house. The rubber coaster gently holds your glass to the table and your table to the glass. The rubber mat holds your wet shoes to the floor while easing your tired legs and feet.

Even when you don't think it's there, rubber often is, hiding under rugs to hold them in position and providing a cushion beneath the wall-to-wall carpet. It is a doorstop, protects wooden floors from being scratched, and door knobs from wrecking walls. It can be a tiny buffer under vases, chairs, and tables, holding them secure yet allowing some play. It works as a sound insulator, muffling vibration from kitchen gadgets.

a way of life

From the simplicity of the rubber band, to the practicality of the tire, the sophistication of designer vases to the comfort of foam-rubber cushioning, rubber is around in every room of the house.

Rubber vases may seem like the product of a perfect marriage, but they are surprisingly rare. This collection displays a variety of natural rubber and silicone vases, including the amusing "Sponge" vase by French company Pylones [bottom left], which makes a wide range of witty rubber products.

Polyurethane rubber
Soft Urn by
Hella Jongerius for
Droog Design,
the Netherlands.

Cactus salt and pepper
containers by Nuvo, USA.

By Maze, USA, makes these white
rubber pills for holding incense,
designed by Assembly. The Think
Plant by RedBox [below], a
meditative cocktail stick holder, is
another of the company's innovations.

WATER BOTTLES

were one of the first industrial uses for rubber. They can hold either hot water or ice for therapeutic effect, and come in a range of shapes for the neck, head, and other sore parts. These vintage bottles, including an early Goodyear patent model from around 1860 [right], display the detail and craftsmanship of the early rubber industry.

Form follows function: this bottle wraps around the neck.

The "Warm Duck" [top left] and "Warm Frog" are two of the novelty hot water bottles by Decor Craft, New York.

Hard rubber syringe from the 19th century.

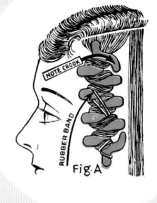

This vintage wig-powdering syringe illustrates how little bulb syringes have changed in design since first being developed by the tribes of South America.

BALDWIN *modern* MARCELLERS

Marcel My Curly

The popular wavy hairstyles of the 1930s were difficult to achieve, and often created by forming the curves with fingers. These Marcellers simply set the hair by twisting it around rubber forms and holding hair in place with an elastic band until it was dry.

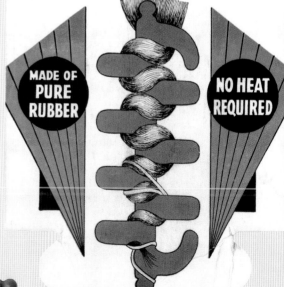

MADE OF PURE RUBBER

NO HEAT REQUIRED

PAT. 1224249   OTHER PATENTS PENDING

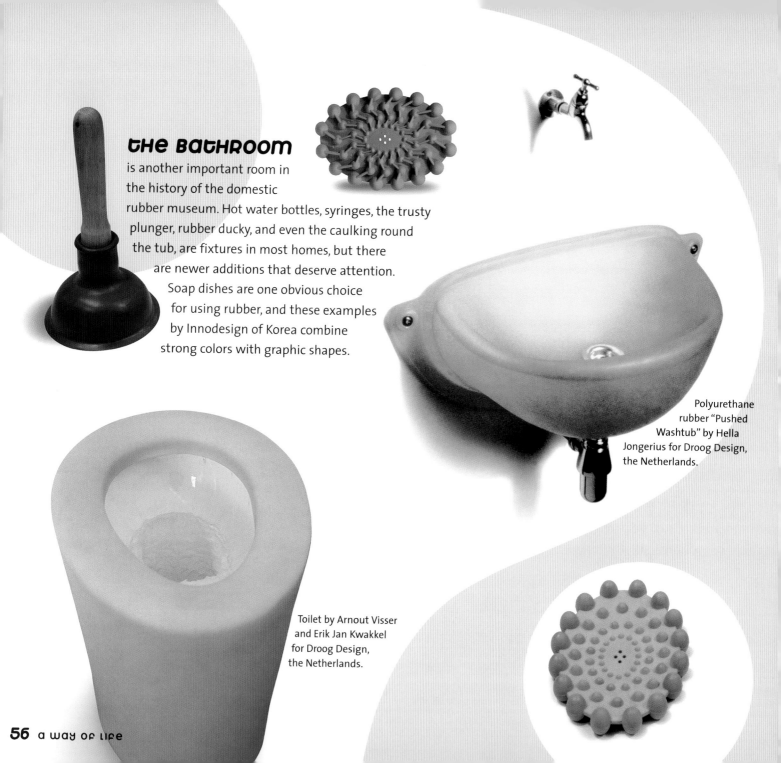

the bathroom

is another important room in the history of the domestic rubber museum. Hot water bottles, syringes, the trusty plunger, rubber ducky, and even the caulking round the tub, are fixtures in most homes, but there are newer additions that deserve attention. Soap dishes are one obvious choice for using rubber, and these examples by Innodesign of Korea combine strong colors with graphic shapes.

Polyurethane rubber "Pushed Washtub" by Hella Jongerius for Droog Design, the Netherlands.

Toilet by Arnout Visser and Erik Jan Kwakkel for Droog Design, the Netherlands.

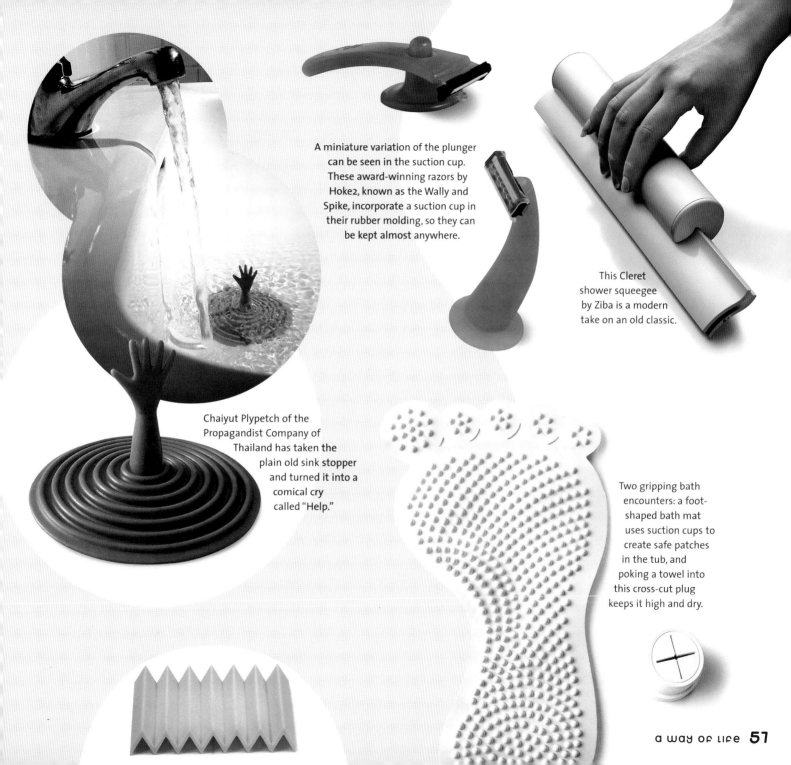

A miniature variation of the plunger can be seen in the suction cup. These award-winning razors by Hoke2, known as the Wally and Spike, incorporate a suction cup in their rubber molding, so they can be kept almost anywhere.

This Cleret shower squeegee by Ziba is a modern take on an old classic.

Chaiyut Plypetch of the Propagandist Company of Thailand has taken the plain old sink stopper and turned it into a comical cry called "Help."

Two gripping bath encounters: a foot-shaped bath mat uses suction cups to create safe patches in the tub, and poking a towel into this cross-cut plug keeps it high and dry.

The spaghetti runner, by Axel Pauli of Belgium, is the perfect backdrop for this Danish ice bucket. Designed by Claus Jensen and Henrik Kolbaek, and made by Tools for Eva Solo, the bucket's lid acts as an ice mold.

Photo: Tomo Futaishi

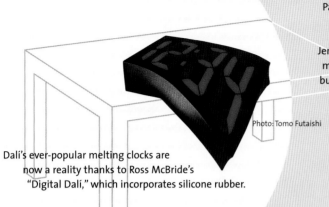

Dalí's ever-popular melting clocks are now a reality thanks to Ross McBride's "Digital Dalí," which incorporates silicone rubber.

Photo: Kozo Takayama

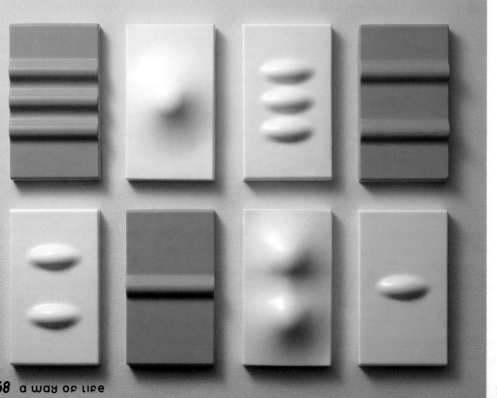

Straps by Droog Design, the Netherlands.

Silicone switches by Ross McBride at Normal.

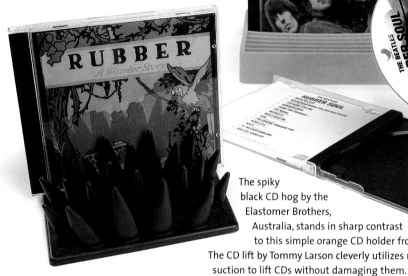

The spiky black CD hog by the Elastomer Brothers, Australia, stands in sharp contrast to this simple orange CD holder from Ikea. The CD lift by Tommy Larson cleverly utilizes rubber's natural suction to lift CDs without damaging them.

Some designers use rubber for no other reason than its aesthetic appeal. The choice of rubber for these articles suggests a desire to express rubber's tactile qualities, although the rubber radio also makes use of its flexible nature in the thin molded membrane that covers the loudspeaker and vibrates accordingly.

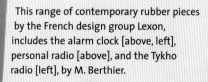

This range of contemporary rubber pieces by the French design group Lexon, includes the alarm clock [above, left], personal radio [above], and the Tykho radio [left], by M. Berthier.

Colorshaper silicone brushes by Forshine and Starr International Ltd provide variety in the manipulation of paint, clay, and other art materials.

The rubber blades of this 1930s Safeflex fan by Samson freed it from the wire cage required on other fans.

Swiss-designed Flexily pen.

The Ion expanding gel pen by Cross has a soft rubber grip.

The Molly Pen (with bent tip) by Prospero Rasulo of Italy, and bright silicone pens with aluminum by Xonex, USA.

The rubber stamp is a simple and indispensable office accessory that has held its own even in the face of modern technology.

W2, UK, makes this silicone rubber "Round Tidy" pen holder, designed by Jackie Piper and Victoria Whitbread.

As great an improvement over the old-style wood base stamp, as the automobile over horse-drawn vehicles!

The twist and wrap "Wiresnake" by Jeff Shore is a Danish answer to cable control. The earlier "Cable Turtle" has inspired vinyl versions such as this 1996 version by Dutch designers Flex Development [below], which organizes and stores excess cable inside its flip shell.

Patented in 1845, the rubber band directly touches the lives of more people than any other rubber creation. It holds together bunches of stuff and, unlike string, automatically adjusts itself to the task at hand, be it letters, hair, or asparagus. These colorful rubber-band animals by Masonori Haneda and Yumiko Ohashi of Passkey Design, Tokyo, give a new twist to an old classic.

These rubber fingertips were developed to help sort through papers.

Olivetti's calculator "Divisumma 18" by Mario Bellini combines rubber and plastic in this 1973 precursor of modern keypads.

"Divisumma 18" courtesy of Cooper-Hewitt National Design Museum, Smithsonian Institution; photo: Matt Flynn.

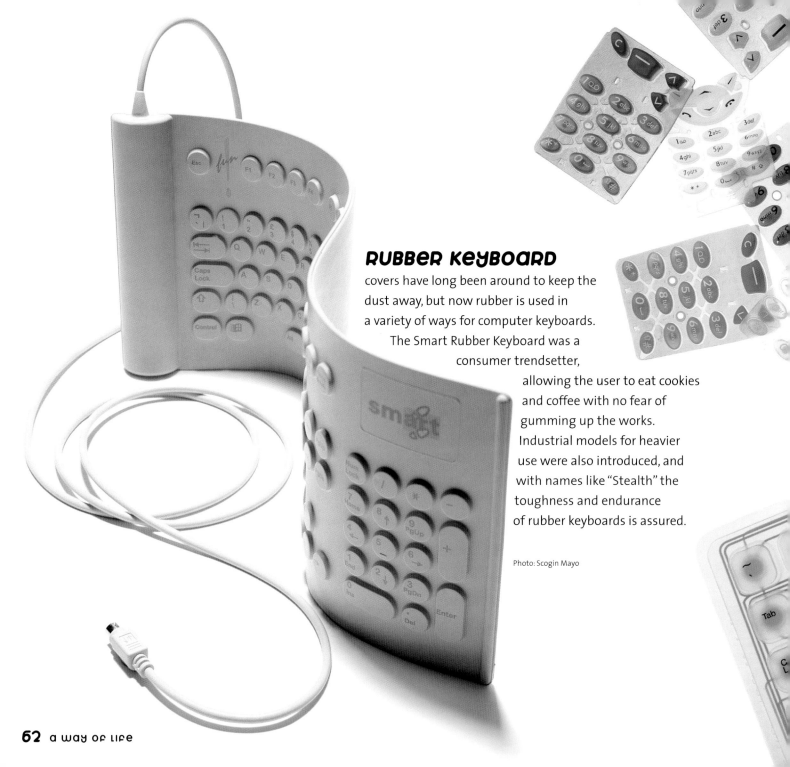

RUBBER KEYBOARD

covers have long been around to keep the dust away, but now rubber is used in a variety of ways for computer keyboards. The Smart Rubber Keyboard was a consumer trendsetter, allowing the user to eat cookies and coffee with no fear of gumming up the works. Industrial models for heavier use were also introduced, and with names like "Stealth" the toughness and endurance of rubber keyboards is assured.

Photo: Scogin Mayo

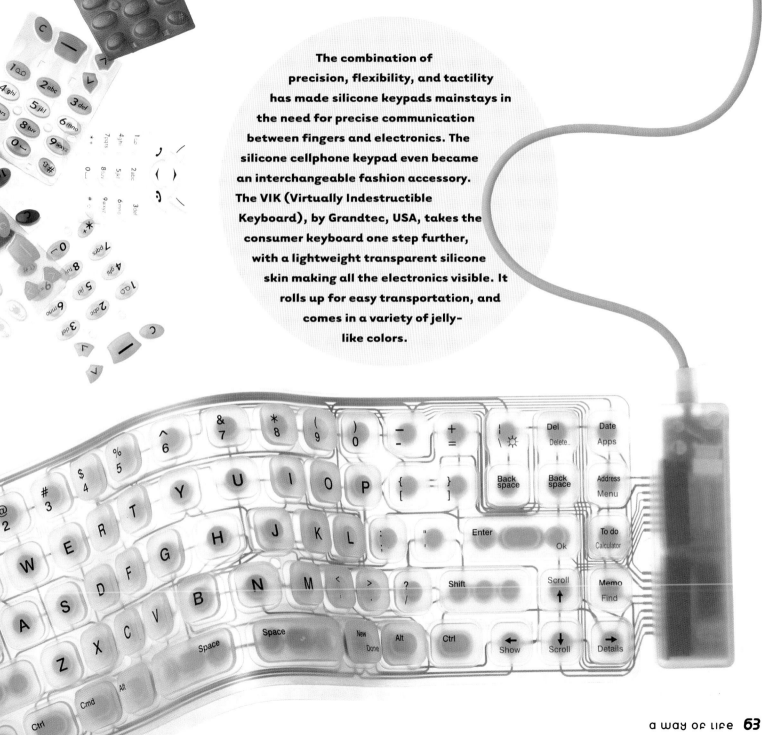

The combination of precision, flexibility, and tactility has made silicone keypads mainstays in the need for precise communication between fingers and electronics. The silicone cellphone keypad even became an interchangeable fashion accessory. The VIK (Virtually Indestructible Keyboard), by Grandtec, USA, takes the consumer keyboard one step further, with a lightweight transparent silicone skin making all the electronics visible. It rolls up for easy transportation, and comes in a variety of jelly-like colors.

Here's a toast to the champagne of the rubber world: foam rubber. Infused with millions of tiny bubbles, this latex froth yields a permanent rubber bubble brew. Developed by Dunlop in 1929, it can be molded, carved, and cast into innumerable shapes. It can soak up water like a sponge through a network of interconnected cells (open cell foam) or be manufactured to float, by closing the cells.

DUNLOP

Leaders of progress in Rubber

Inventor of the first practical pneumatic tyre and founder of the latex foam industry, Dunlop for three generations has played a major part in research and development associated with rubber and its allied industries. Today the great Dunlop Research Centre at Fort Dunlop carries on the Dunlop tradition of service and progress

DUNLOP PRODUCTS ARE MANUFACTURED IN ARGENTINA · AUSTRALIA · BRAZIL · CANADA · ENGLAND · FRANCE · GERMANY · INDIA · REPUBLIC OF ... NEW ZEALAND · PERU · SOUTH AFRICA · SWEDEN AND USA · BRANCHES AND DISTRIBUTORS THROUGHOUT THE WORLD

The curvaceous Fannyette logo on this stadium-style seating mat from 1939 says it all. A forerunner to modern foam seating, kneeling pads, exercise mats, and sports protection gear, thin foam of varying densities has become a cushioning classic.

Light and malleable, mildew resistant, and bug free, foam rubber has many advantages. It cushions the ears when used as a sound absorber, and its range of textures can form patterns on walls and padding under carpets. The bubbles trapped in the fabric-like layers of neoprene rubber keep scuba divers warm in the ocean. Line an entire room with foam rubber and you have your own padded cell — the ultimate in safety and protection.

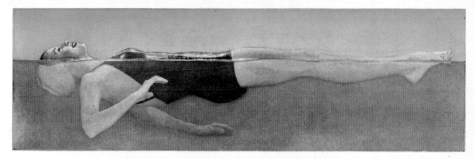

AS YOU FLOAT ON WATER

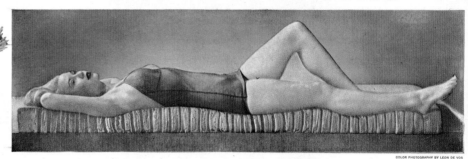

YOU "FLOAT" ON KOYLON FOAM

Foam rubber's molecular makeup – a union of billions of minuscule balloons – creates mattresses that provide unparalleled support, resistance, and comfort.

Cushy Number of Scotland extends the use of latex by casting a cushion cover to resemble a soft lawn of chubby latex fibers.

These massage rollers from the 1930s were equipped with textured surfaces that gently kneaded the skin. The green-handled electric version from 1932 also produces therapeutic heat.

IN THE LATE 19TH CENTURY, a Belfast veterinarian named John Boyd Dunlop patented a pneumatic tire for his son's tricycle. During the gay 1890s, when bicycles were all the rage, people enjoyed the freedom that cycling afforded. Bicycles were, in fact, the reason tires were invented.

The cycling craze was not only the basis for major developments in the tire industry, but also created such a massive market for tires that the big companies like Firestone were able to establish themselves and their products well before Henry Ford created the need for production-line quantities in the early 20th century.

When cars finally raced on to the scene, the tire industry's foundation had been set. The volume of motorcar traffic, which shaped the American landscape after 1909, boosted rubber consumption yet again, and transformed Akron, Ohio, into the "Rubber Capital of the World."

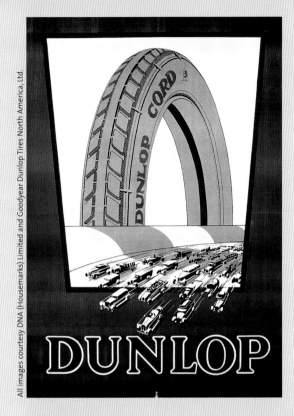

ALTHOUGH TIRES are probably the most well-known use of rubber, early manufacturers were eager to educate people about the variety of automotive uses. As well as producing a variety of stylish tire ads, they promoted road building and auto accessories, which were equally big business.

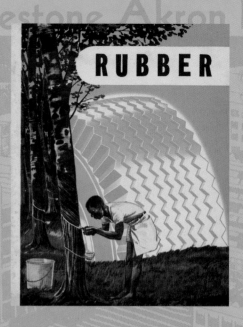

RUBBER

The MIRACLE of RUBBER

"DEATH DODGER" JIMMIE LYNCH TESTS B. F. GOODRICH TIRES —

THE ROADS AND HIGHWAYS ARE THEIR PROVING GROUNDS AND DAREDEVIL DRIVER JIMMIE LYNCH OF WORLD'S FAIR FAME GIVES B.F. GOODRICH SILVERTOWN TIRES THAT EXTRA SPECIAL TEST.

THERE GOES A HUB CAP!

JIMMY PUTS THEM THROUGH THEIR PACES AT DAYTONA BEACH, FLORIDA. HE BURNS UP THE SANDS AT HIGH SPEEDS, SCREAMS INTO SPINNING SKIDS, THEN RACES OVER A STRETCH OF RAILROAD TIES.

NEWEST B.F. GOODRICH TIRE HAS NO INNER TUBE AND WILL SEAL PUNCTURES ON THE ROLLING WHEEL. HERE IS THE TUBELESS TIRE UNDERGOING A SPIKEBOARD TEST.

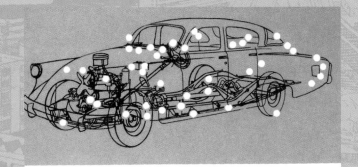

1   Half the rubber in a car is off the ground. Besides tires, a car has 350 rubber parts, including wiring, foam cushions and fan belt.

Firestone

TIRES FOR EVERY PURSE AND PURPOSE

PASSENGER TIRES
Including Complete Line
of Tubeless Tires

Blowout
Life Protector

TRUCK TIRES   FARM TIRES

As in this classic advertising ashtray, miniature tires were produced by most major rubber companies as promotional items.

The standard garage houses not only a car, but also a range of rubbery devices. Latex-based paint, introduced in 1857, is still around. Garden hoses, once made of rubber, are now usually made of vinyl. Classic rubber flashlights, such as these made by Decor Craft, New York, come in myriad colors, and dog toys abound. The Blue Ribbon Dog Co. dreamt up the stylish cubist bone, and even Gucci developed a dog frisbee. The "fly" takes the ball one step further by adding a plastic reed that gives the signature "buzz" when thrown.

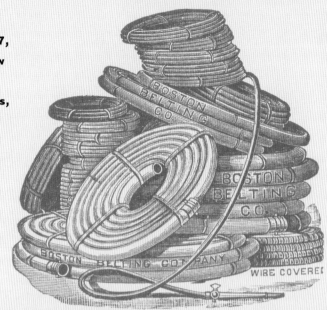

ACCURATE rubber tape

Whereas plastic tape is rigid, rubber tape has "give." Consequently, it can also be used as a sealant.

Foam animals make excellent hand exercisers. Since rubber always matches the strength of its user, it's the perfect material for providing resistance. The earliest elastic exercise machine was patented in 1853.

The clothes wringer was a pioneering timesaving device. The rubber rollers are still used in many parts of the world.

Combination lock and tape measure by Lexon.

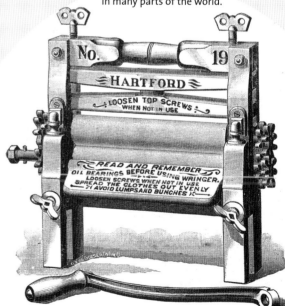

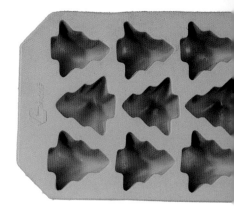

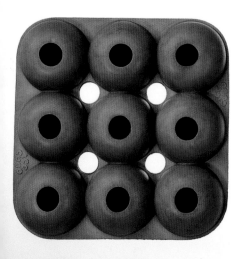

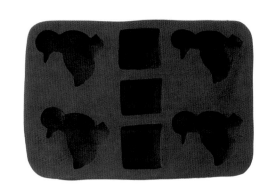

A series of **miniature ice sculptures** are a simple creation with rubber working as your assistant. Complex shapes can be popped intact out of rubber, the Cubo ice maker from the 1940s [far left] made ice balls that could be pushed out from the small holes in the mold. The yellow butter molds [top left] use silicone to replicate delicate leaf or flower patterns in butter. Plastic lacks the flexibility needed to release such intricately molded shapes.

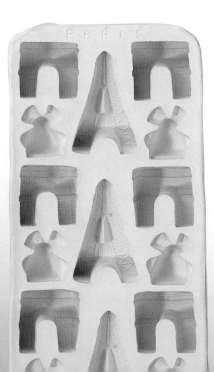

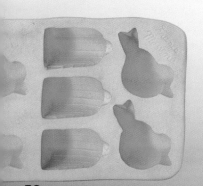

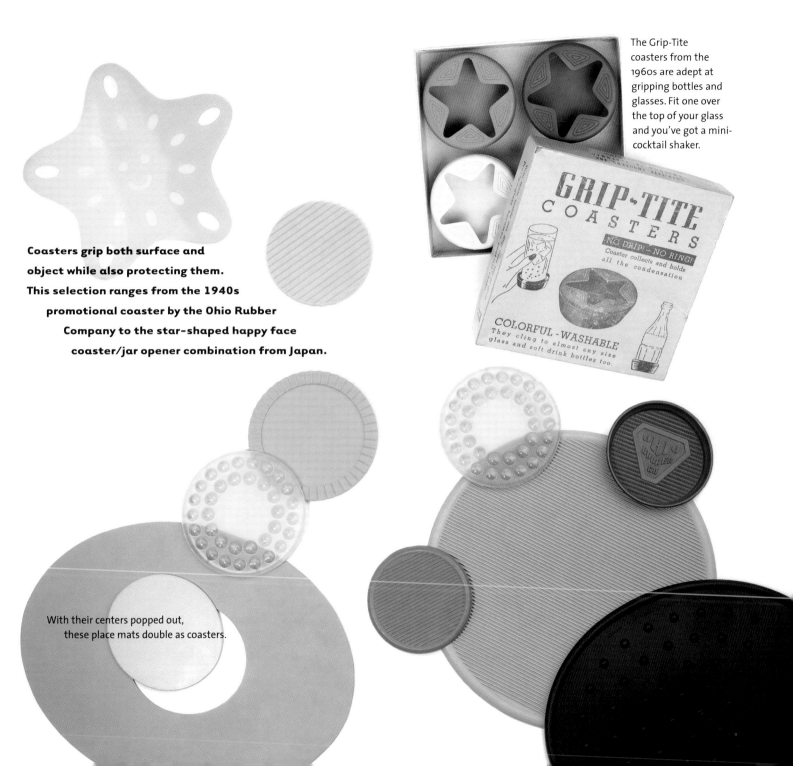

The Grip-Tite coasters from the 1960s are adept at gripping bottles and glasses. Fit one over the top of your glass and you've got a mini-cocktail shaker.

Coasters grip both surface and object while also protecting them. This selection ranges from the 1940s promotional coaster by the Ohio Rubber Company to the star-shaped happy face coaster/jar opener combination from Japan.

GRIP-TITE
C O A S T E R S
NO DRIP! – NO RING!
Coaster collects and holds all the condensation

COLORFUL - WASHABLE
They cling to almost any size glass and soft drink bottles too.

With their centers popped out, these place mats double as coasters.

The introduction of rubber gaskets in the mid-19th century revolutionized food preservation at home.

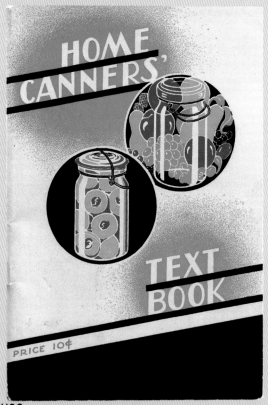

RUBBER GLOVES were first patented in the 1850s. They gained popularity in the 1890s when surgeons began using them to protect their hands from dangerous substances. It was only later that they became a standard appliance for maintaining a sterile environment.

Silicone rubber withstands up to about 400° Fahrenheit, so it's the perfect choice for cake pans. Cakes bake more evenly when there's no metal to overheat the edges.

This garlic peeler is essentially a silicone tube for rapidly rolling off garlic skins.

Spatulas now come in silicone in jelly-like colors and work just as well as the latex type.

The Rubbermaid Company was launched in 1933 and evolved into a leading name in housewares. The maid on this vintage mat represented a big help in the kitchen.

The non-stick nature of silicone makes the Silpat mat perfect for rolling out pastry.

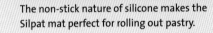

DOPPELGÄNGER

Famous as a mold maker, rubber possesses an eerie capacity to mimic other forms and substances, giving it a strange place in contemporary existence. It's the magic and the magician, the trickster and the trick. What you thought was real is only an old friend who's incredibly adept at appearing to be what it isn't. And it's in the replication department that rubber performs its greatest work, either as the means to an end or as the end product itself. In art, what's not there is just as important as what is. A sculpture does not exist without negative space. It is the sculptor's skill in creating the space around a shape that gets our attention. And although there may be no rubber in this hypothetical sculpture, it very likely helped to create it,

In the prototype for flexible picnicware by Olmeca, USA [right], the shape of the rubber-tree leaf has been used, making a flexible "plate" that is easy to hold in one hand. Cast in natural rubber, the leaf imitates life not only in its form, but also with its DNA.

DOPPELGÄNGER

because rubber is the primary choice of artists and technicians when casting and mold making. This is the silent aspect of rubber's artistic abilities.

But here again, rubber's achievement is in not being noticed. Does rubber itself ever get to be in the spotlight? Occasionally, a well-placed rubber article will be portrayed in a painting in such a way as to bring attention to itself. Giorgio de Chirico incorporated the rubber glove in his surreal vision of the world. But there are some artists and professions that rely heavily on the imitative qualities of rubber, and the success of their work can frequently be measured only by the extent to which it goes unnoticed. This is true for all included in this section, and particularly for people who depend on prosthetics, as rubber can directly change their lives.

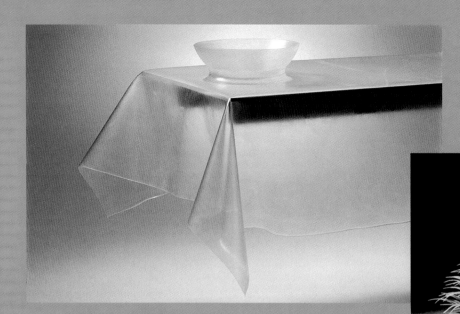

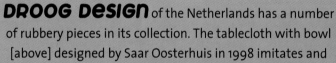

DROOG DESIGN of the Netherlands has a number of rubbery pieces in its collection. The tablecloth with bowl [above] designed by Saar Oosterhuis in 1998 imitates and combines two items into one soft polyurethane unit, and the Artificial Plant, 1995, by Frank Tjepkema [above right] combines plastic with rubber to make a surreal indoor plant decoration.

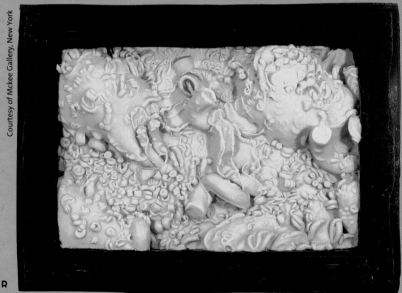

Jeannie Silverthorne is an artist who uses rubber as her medium. In this piece, *Ulcer, Bacteria Promoting*, 2000, rubber is used to create the "feel" of body parts. Her frames are also modeled from latex.

Multi-colored 10 inch zippers, 2000, zippers and rubber.

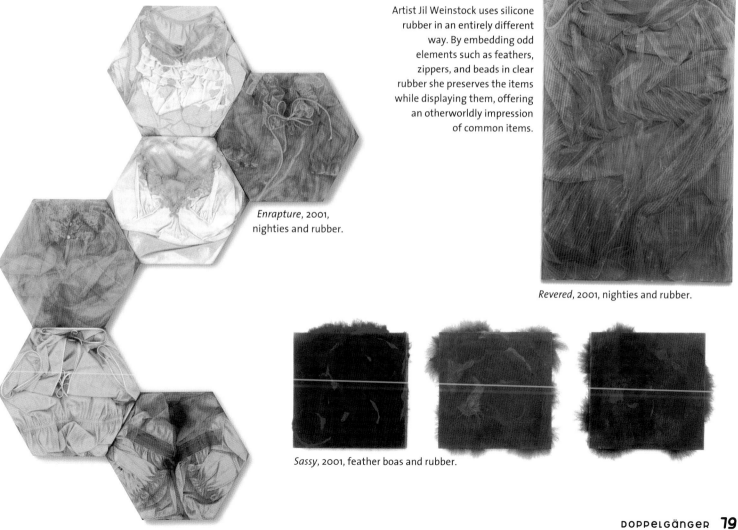

Artist Jil Weinstock uses silicone rubber in an entirely different way. By embedding odd elements such as feathers, zippers, and beads in clear rubber she preserves the items while displaying them, offering an otherworldly impression of common items.

Enrapture, 2001, nighties and rubber.

Revered, 2001, nighties and rubber.

Sassy, 2001, feather boas and rubber.

Long before genetic engineers were cloning vegetables, rubber was the leader in the cloning business. On close inspection these potatoes made by Iwamatsu are identical. They feel and weigh the same as the real thing. The company also makes believable bananas [below].

This rubber lump of cheese is actually a silicone paperweight and pencil organizer by By Maze, USA. It can also be used as a doorstop.

On the set of *A Perfect Storm*, angry animal rights activists were surprised to learn that the flapping fish on the dock were rubber animatronic fakes. This fishy pencil case by Nadel Patte of Germany could not be mistaken for the real thing.

The cabbage is brought to life by a different technique; painted fabric leaves are dipped in natural latex, simulating the feel of the real thing.

Humans are not the only ones to be fooled by rubber. Fishermen have long used rubber to trick and catch their prey. The vintage brown rubber lures have stiffened, but the modern varieties incorporate silicone fringe skirts and light-catching glitter, thus moving with the agility of accomplished swimmers.

GHE PROSGHEGICS AND HOLLYWOOD

special effects industries have similar goals, to imitate life, but they have entirely different sets of requirements. Hollywood uses rubber in many ways; the scale can range from the dinosaurs of *Jurassic Park* to a small prosthetic nose that can completely alter an actor's appearance. These effects need to fool the public in close-up, and the best are ones no one ever notices. Created for one scene or a six-week shoot, these relatively short-term solutions don't necessarily translate when developing appliances for repetitive human usage. Visual appeal may not be as vital for prosthetic functionality, but it is important for the psyche of the wearer. A fake body part must fool onlookers for at least the first few seconds to help its owner fit in comfortably with society at large.

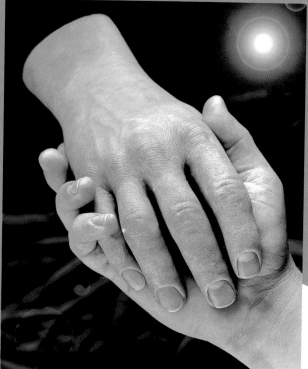

Courtesy of Alatheia Prosthetics

Alatheia's Dermatos Prosthesis

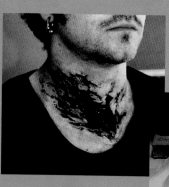

Gary Tunnicliffe uses the more traditional foam latex to create this neck scar effect.

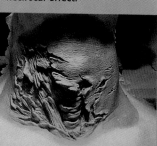

The case of Clint Hallam illustrates that prosthetics are not necessarily inferior to the real thing. The beneficiary of the first human hand transplant later found a surgeon who would remove it. Among other issues, he complained of feeling as though it didn't "belong" to him. He chose prosthetics as being preferable to a real, foreign hand on his arm.

American Civil War injuries created a demand for artificial limbs at the time India rubber was being developed. In 1862, Thomas White patented artificial limbs made from rubber, and in 1865, Amasa Marks produced affordable legs at $65 each. The cosmetic dental industry depends heavily on hard rubber, for both teeth and reconstructive surgery.

Make-up artist Gordon Smith has created a
vast number of effects. Included here are:
a totally artificial man, made of silicone,
a polyurethane rubber monkey, and the
first old-age silicone prosthetic, made
using a new silicone technique he
developed, which set new standards
in make-up design.

Victorian ladies could purchase **INDIA·RUBBER "FALSITIES"** (later known as "falsies"), which were patented in 1867. For much of the following century, foam rubber was used for shoulder and bust pads, but the advent of silicone gels has revolutionized the bosom business. Initially developed for breast cancer victims, mastectomy products have become a smash hit with women from all walks of life. In some cases, silicone is worn inside a bra, giving both wearer and observer a feel for the weight and movement of real breasts. For those who want to carry the illusion further, surgical implants are the ultimate option. Although bad publicity has slowed the use of silicone breast implants, replacing it with other substances, they have recently been reintroduced, and silicone outerwear remains a safe and satisfactory way to make use of its finer attributes.

In 1863 William Elmer first patented his version of artificial leather, though similar methods had been around for centuries. This modern "Treetap" bag uses local labor to make vegetal artificial leather from native South American rubber trees. This vegetal material has even been used by Hermès, Paris.

This bag by Furla, Italy, is one molded rubber piece. All the stitching details have been faithfully reproduced to create the form and style of a leather bag.

The Spenco Medical Corporation's "Nearly Me" line of silicone breasts and breast enhancers include a range of mastectomy products that have been adopted by many others who also wish to make the illusion realistic.

In contrast to the all-rubber bag, Argentinian artist Nicola Costantino combines silicone rubber human nipples with leather to produce an eerie result: human skin bags. These Human Furrier pieces are surprisingly similar to their ostrich counterparts.

Courtesy of Deitch Projects, New York

If you want a custom-made dominatrix, you'll have to close your eyes and pretend. But if you're looking for an agreeable, docile beauty, silicone hasn't left much to the imagination. State-of-the-art silicone playmates blur fantasy and reality in the bedroom as the best technology from the film and prosthetics industries have been combined to fill a niche in the market for high-end sex dolls. Boasting the "World's Finest Love Doll," the Real Doll Company custom-builds full-sized flavorless, odorless sex kittens to personal specification — from body size and color right down to eyeshadow hue and hairstyle. The company uses silicone rubber of varying firmness to achieve this grand illusion, incorporating gel-like silicone in places such as the breasts while using firmer textures for feet and elbows. Rubber's natural qualities also lend the doll's orifices unsurpassed suction, while urethane foam, vinyl skeletons, and steel joints provide flexible positioning. These love dolls weigh as much as their human counterparts, and they even have internal hand armatures, enabling them to grip and hold.

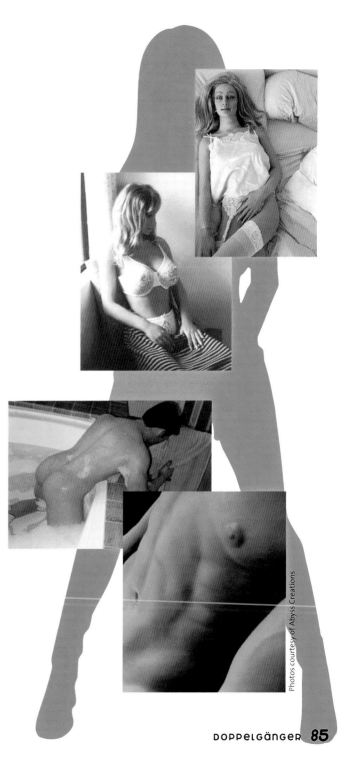

Photos courtesy of Abyss Creations

Mojo by Myla, UK, is a silicone rubber five-speed vibrating toy designed by Marc Newson. It is available in two color combinations, orange/pink and blue/green.

RUBBER BANNED

Discovering the erotic world of rubber is like exploring an amusement park full of wild rides and colorful attractions, but this ride is for adults only, and it travels through some bizarre territory. Having covered rubber's capacity for simulation, we now move into the arena of stimulation, although the two concepts frequently overlap. Have a look around, there are things to boggle the mind and spark the senses. There are the more traditional rubber female contraceptives, and then, of course, the condom, which has always been the mainstay of disease prevention, and arrived in enormous numbers and varieties in response to the AIDS crisis of the 1980s. Consequently, ordering a condom these days is like asking Starbucks for a coffee, the size, strength, color, texture, function, and aesthetic appeal of the product are all part of the choice. The current rainbow of adult toys can be difficult to tell apart from some of the stranger playthings in a toyshop. The local sex shop, however, suffers fierce competition from the Internet, which expands the horizons of the mail-order adventurer too reserved to wander into a public store. This is a journey into a new realm and, in this case, the journey is as significant as the destination.

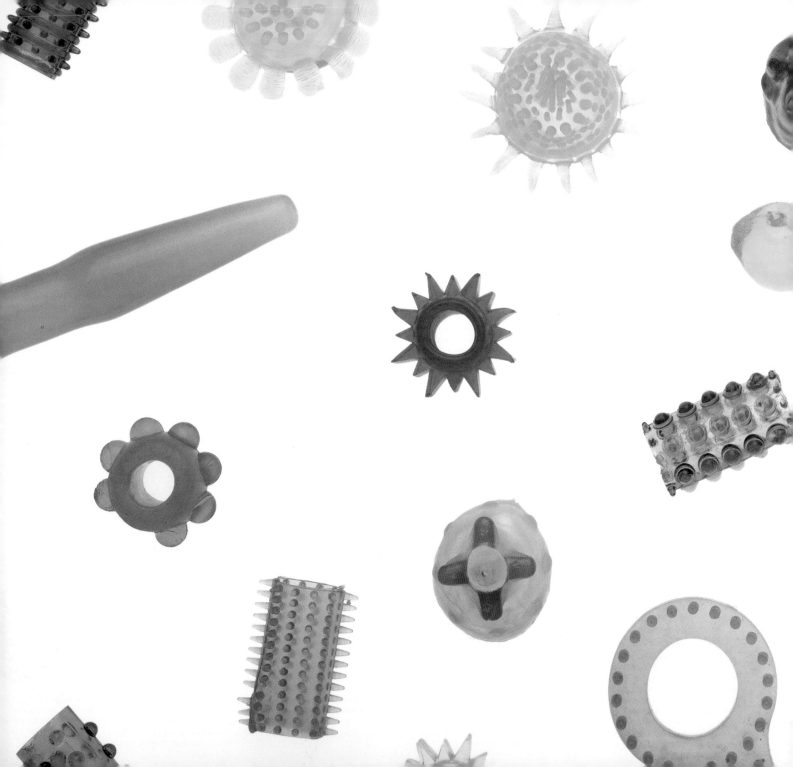

CONDOMS have been around for centuries (there are even surviving samples from 1640), but the rubber variety is relatively new. Contraceptive reliability wasn't the main function of the condom, as evidenced by the lax enforcement of safety standards before 1987. Until then, the condom was defined in the US as a class 2 medical device, and there were no recalls. Then came the turning point, when the condom was upgraded to a "life saving device," and the FDA tested more than 54,000 of them over several months, developing and enforcing the safety standards enjoyed today. In becoming a better lifesaver, it has improved as a life-preventer as well.

Condoms have become a modern fashion accessory, with designer labels and rock-star endorsements. Prince played on the title of his popular movie and album, packaging his "Purple Raincoats" in a CD-style box, with a wink to Casanova's age-old reference to "English overcoats."

Mrs Phillips: her name was to condoms what Kleenex is to tissues, yet there appear to have been not one, but a few Mrs Phillips. In 1776, this British brand covered the world, with sales pitches like: "to gard yourself from shame or fear. Votaries to venus, hasten here; None in our wares e'er found a flaw, self-preservation's nature's law," (letters-post paid duly answered).

The breaking point: in case you care to measure, the modern condom legally must be between 0.03mm and 0.09mm thick. Most US varieties have a thickness of 0.04mm – the world's tiniest security guards. They must have an integral rim, be 150–200mm long, 47–54mm wide, and not weigh more than 2 grams. They must reach a stretching-point of 625% before breaking (sounds neat, but don't try that one at home). They have a 4% failure rate due to dimensions, 2.5% due to strength and elongation, and 0.4% due to leakage.

Sausage skin manufacturer Julius Schmid took his talents to the next obvious step, providing hand-dipped latex condoms in the US in the early 20th century. Schmid Labs eventually consolidated with the Young Rubber Company, makers of the popular Trojan brand, leading to control of over 84% of the market by the mid-1930s.

Mary had a little lambskin: Casanova used lamb intestines, meticulously prepared and bordered at the opening with a ribbon. He provides detailed information on their use in his *Histoire de la Vie*, and he is credited with popularizing them with men and women, blowing them up, and describing the "English overcoats" as "the little preventative bags invented by the English to save the fair sex from anxiety." It would be another 150 years before the rubber version poked its way into the industry.

This condom container [below] displays the smooth-as-silk quality of the condoms inside with both its name and the surface texture of the tin.

Women's contraceptives have also witnessed rubber replacing age-old devices like sponges and natural diaphragms. The sponge was the obvious forerunner to this modern Protectaid contraceptive sponge. Like its popular 18th-century predecessor (which was saturated with water and a little brandy), the sponge is ideal for retaining potions, thanks to its absorbent texture. Another ancient device was a squeezed lemon half, used as a cervical cap, which translated beautifully into the rubber diaphragm. Both the Lea and the crystal clear Oves pictured here are rubbery variations of the diaphragm method.

"The Keeper" is a natural rubber collection cup and a simple reusable alternative to tampons.

RUBBER'S VaLue

RUBBER'S VaLue for intimate wear was not limited to making contraceptives; the garment industry had disciples enamored with the new waterproof material of the 19th century. Raincoats, shoes, and gloves were staples of the rubber industry, and spawned the creation of one of the world's oldest fetish organizations. The Mackintosh Society, well established by the early 1900s, provided a network by which rubber devotees could keep in touch, becoming the foundation for the more mainstream rubber fetishist-fashion crossovers that found their way into popular culture by the 1960s.

Hard-rubber (vulcanite) pipe from the early 20th century.

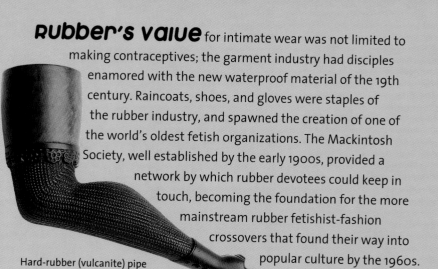

This Candee Rubber Company card from 1907 offers a mixed message. The gents at the Rubber Club are obviously ogling the passing ladies, but the connotations of such a "club" could be interpreted in a number of ways here. The rubber fetishist was well established by 1907, though it is doubtful that the Candee Rubber Company was aiming at this market, unless the nod-nod, wink-wink mentality was already attached to rubber by this time. The intricately made miniature boots and glove are vintage salesman's samples.

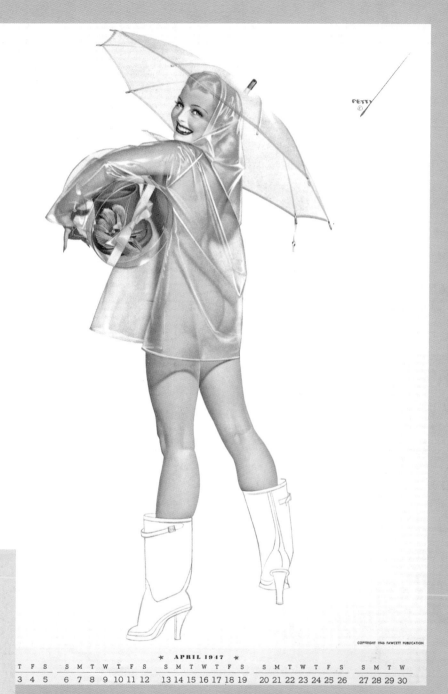

In the mid-1940s, Goodrich researchers developed Koroseal, a transparent rubber hydrochloride film, casting a new light on rubber development. Synthetics developed quickly, and plastics have surpassed rubber in volume. Used as a saucy outfit on this 1947 pin-up girl, the sexy future of rubber and plastics was becoming assured. The only opaque garment on this girl is her pair of rubber boots.

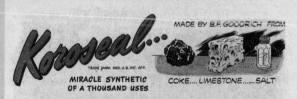
★ APRIL 1947 ★

T	F	S		S	M	T	W	T	F	S		S	M	T	W	T	F	S		S	M	T	W	T	F	S		S	M	T	W
3	4	5		6	7	8	9	10	11	12		13	14	15	16	17	18	19		20	21	22	23	24	25	26		27	28	29	30

COPYRIGHT 1946 FAWCETT PUBLICATION

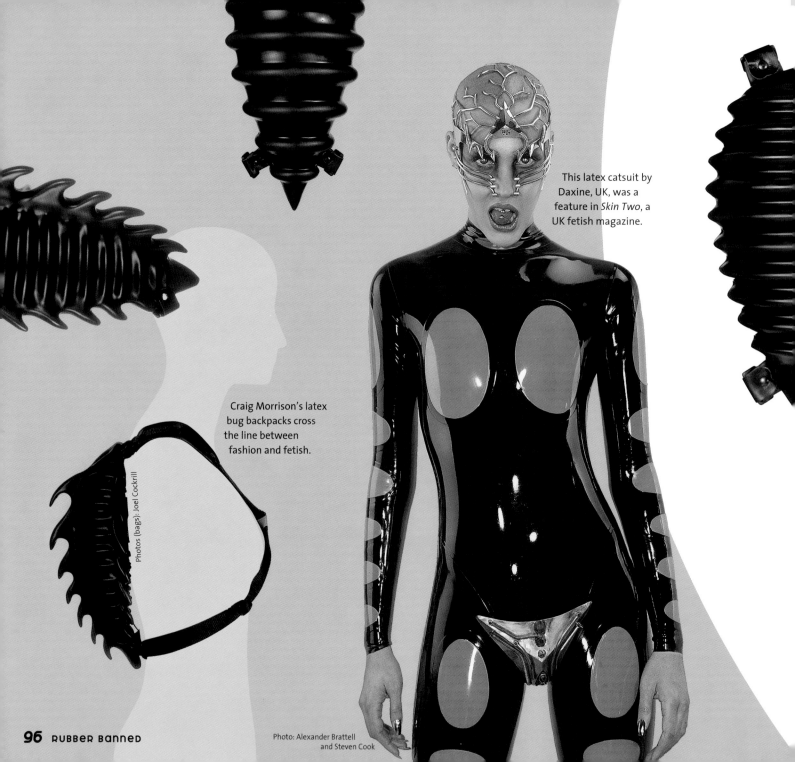

This latex catsuit by Daxine, UK, was a feature in *Skin Two*, a UK fetish magazine.

Craig Morrison's latex bug backpacks cross the line between fashion and fetish.

Photos (bags): Joel Cockrill

Photo: Alexander Brattell and Steven Cook

FOCUS is the essence of fetish. The totality of the body gives way to a single stirring feature or accessory. For rubber fetishists it is the sensory explosion delivered by being enclosed in rubber, the grip, shine, squeak, and the lack of breathability. This shot by Peter Ashworth, "Girl on a Spikey Settee," was a trendsetter in 1990. It was the starting point for real fetish in the mainstream. Fashion pages in the 1960s had seen the beginning of the crossover with shiny vinyl trousers and coats, and characters such as Catwoman and Emma Peel popularized these styles, but it had never been quite as explicit as in this shot for MTV.

Latex couch by Craig Morrison.

GIANT STEPS

Man never actually set foot on the moon, rubber
did. And it left its sprawling signature for the universe to
see in the form of wiggling tire tracks, punctuated by a few well-
placed boot prints.

Some of our vehicles remained on the moon's surface, including the first
rubber lunar tires, made by Goodyear and delivered on Apollo 14. Those tires wait
among the silent craters as a reminder of the piles of unwanted tires here on earth.
Do we want the moon to be an overflow dumping ground for the pollution we have no
place for at home? Do we want earth to become a trash heap, for that matter? Will the
Great Wall of Steel-Belted Radials be the next man-made achievement visible from outer
space? Rubber is certainly not our only (or worst) waste disposal problem,
but it's a good place for us to start as we consider planetary
problems and solutions.

The moonwalk left big legacies. For the first time, we
saw the planet as outsiders looking in. We saw the
"oneness" of our total environment – the bigger
picture. It's time we consider rubber as part
of our expanded worldview and
consciousness, and rethink its potential
future and contribution to the
ecology of our planet.

ASTRONAUT SUIT

B. F. GOODRICH IS PROUD TO HAVE DEVELOPED THE SUIT USED BY PROJECT MERCURY ASTRONAUTS FOR OUR NATION'S ENTRY INTO SPACE!

THE WORLD'S FIRST HIGH ALTITUDE SUIT WAS MADE BY B. F. GOODRICH FOR FAMED PILOT WILEY POST IN 1934!

What IS this world coming to?

FLYING WINGS . . . tear-drop cars . . . television . . . electronics . . . plastic houses . . . you can paint your own dream and your guess is apt to be as good as the next fellow's.

Frankly, we don't believe Main Street is going to be transformed into a comic book conception of the planet Saturn as soon as the ink dries on the peace treaties. Sure, we are going to see some pretty quick changes . . . in homes, on farms, in offices, in plants. Changes for the better — better living, better working, better playing — but when, or how soon, a streamlined Utopian world will be complete is just guesswork.

Anyhow, "when" is not the point. The important thing is that we *are* on the way. Progress is already being made . . . and in that progress all of us here at Acushnet expect to have a part.

What we've learned in making materials of rubber and synthetic rubber for the uses of war is going to come in mighty handy later on. Perhaps it's going to help your engine to run a little smoother, or your pump to operate a little more efficiently, or your business machine to wear longer, or your radio to sound sweeter, or your chair to be more comfortable.

Whatever it is and whenever we start, it's all right with us — *after* we finish our war job. And, although rubber parts made by Acushnet may not always be in evidence in the article you buy, there will be many used by many manufacturers who will be turning out many things for your comfort, pleasure* and convenience. Acushnet Process Company, New Bedford, Mass. *Pleasure?—well, come peace, make a date with yourself to tee off with an Acushnet Titleist Golf Ball — post-war model. BUY WAR BONDS — KEEP AMERICA FREE

In rubber, remember the name — **ACUSHNET**

RIDE ON A MOVING RUBBER SIDEWALK-- THE FIRST IN THE WORLD!

Our idea of the future changes with each generation, and the optimism of an era is reflected in that vision. The naïve exuberance of the Space Race created great advancements in technology, which have been transformed into many articles for everyday use. Memory Foam, for example, is a visco-elastic heat sensitive foam, developed by NASA, and has become popular in the bedding industry, providing healthy competition for the more standard polyurethane foam rubber. Images of earth from space also helped launch the modern environmental movement, and the optimism previously centered on technological advancement is now focusing on preservation and renewal, and recycling has become a key player in this new way of thinking.

Expandable moon shelter by Goodyear Aerospace is for possible use in U.S. moon mission.

RUBBER AND THE BIG TOMORROW

What will rubber do for an encore? Well, all the mysteries haven't been tapped and rubber has a future as big as space itself....

This is merely the last page in this booklet, not the last page in the history of rubber. Rubber already has been into space, but the sky is no limit to where it will go.

When men reach the moon, they may live in rubber houses which can be packed into the nose cones of rockets and expanded to room-sized igloos. This same type of collapsible house may first be used in space stations.

Right here on Earth, rubber keeps going like sixty. Medical science will use it to replace vital body organs. Many of today's rubber products will change (and improve) vastly. There simply is no limit.

But rubber will make its most dramatic history in space. There is even the possibility that the first man to get to Mars or some other planet may be greeted by ancient tribesmen who will be bouncing little rubber balls around, not knowing what else to do with them. Sounds familiar, doesn't it?

With an estimated 2.5 to **3 BILLION USED TIRES** waiting in piles in the US alone, recycling presents a sizeable problem. This massive supply of free raw materials has been used, however, by The Earthship Community in New Mexico, who build standardized housing units from old tires. These "Earthships" are structured around dirt-packed tires, which, coated in an adobe type shell, result in cheap, earth-friendly architecture. This simple building method was also incorporated into the stylish structures made from recycled materials that Samuel Mockbee created in poor rural Alabama communities with the aid of his architecture students.

Others have used whole tires in novel ways. During the 1970s, batches of weighted tires were placed on the sea floor as a base for marine growth, with which they quickly became encrusted and so attracted fish. They're surprisingly good at replicating the marine environment of our depleted reefs, though hurricanes have been known to disturb them, washing tires

ashore in some cases. Scrap tires have also been placed in underground rows beneath golf courses. Their forms are ideal for evening out drainage and retaining water to reduce irrigation needs. Highway protection and cushioning on boat docks are other solutions; the Topper Company uses them to make buoys. Cut in half they make excellent bases for traffic cones, and in Florida they are burnt in citrus orchards to save crops from the occasional frost. On an individual level, they have been doctored into amusing planters and tire swings, but until more uses present themselves, tires will be chipped, crumbed and shredded, and turned into something else entirely.

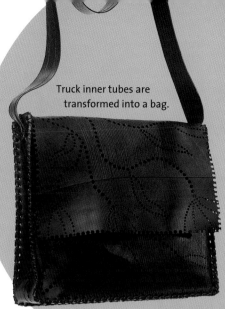

Truck inner tubes are transformed into a bag.

As complicated and expensive as a tire is to make, so it is to reclaim. Re-capping is the simplest and most viable procedure, but this practice tends to be popular only where economic hardship makes it a necessity, but even after re-capping, tires present the same problem when disposal time comes around. Scrap tires have limited uses, but a little ingenuity has given rise to some inspiring visions. Cultural influences, financial necessity, and creative spirit can produce astounding articles from humanity's waste pile. Generally, the poorer the region the more imaginative the results of recycling. This Moroccan water jug is an earth-friendly substitute for the original copper versions, complete with rivets and all the trimmings.

Courtesy of The Museum of International Folk Art, Santa Fé; photo: John Bigelow Taylor.

Some companies create innovative products with tire waste. Shredded tires have been made into bug resistant mulch by Rubberiffic. When mixed with binders, crumb rubber can be formed into a variety of surfaces for roads, playgrounds and farm matting. Tirex makes tough flooring, which is popular for areas that suffer heavy use. Rubber lumber [above] is ideal for use as decking, boat docks, and patios, as it does not require the level of care of wood.

Discarded flip-flops were used by Saarenald T. S. Yaawaisan of Monrovia, Liberia, to make this toy helicopter.

Flip-flop factory waste is used in this doormat from the Philippines.

drink

O.R.E. in California makes a range of coasters and place mats from recycled rubber.

Made of recycled Wellington boots, these coasters also incorporate vinyl.

Used Rubber USA collects and transforms old tires and inner tubes into wallets and bags.

The UK company RE-MARKABLE is famous for its pencils made of styrofoam cups, but these pencil cases and booklet covers [right] show that new recycled rubber material also offers many possibilities.

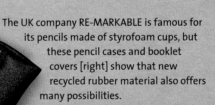

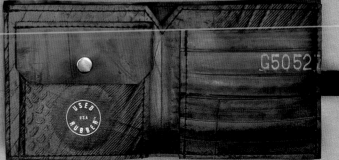

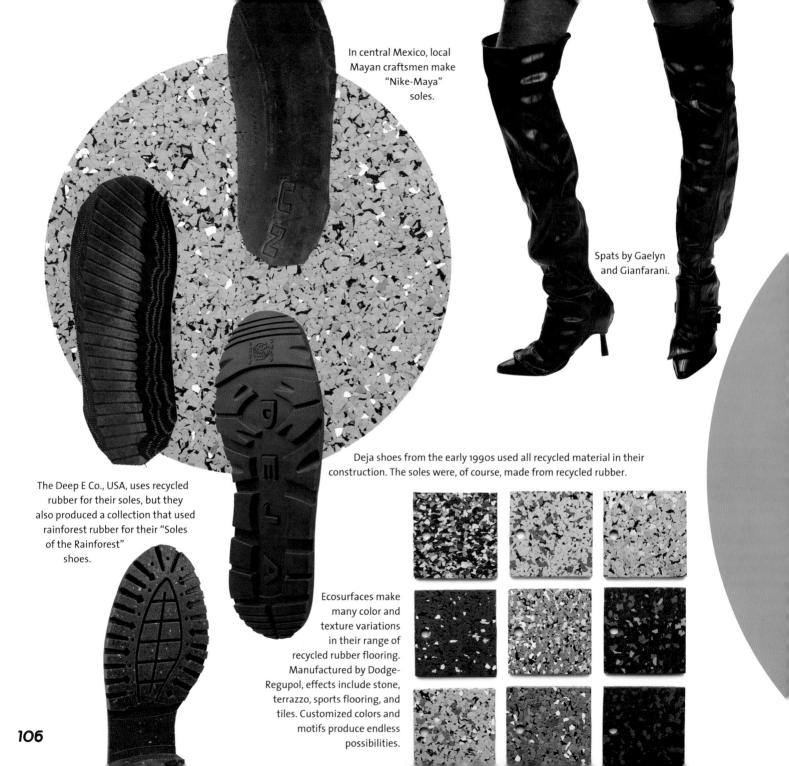

In central Mexico, local Mayan craftsmen make "Nike-Maya" soles.

Spats by Gaelyn and Gianfarani.

The Deep E Co., USA, uses recycled rubber for their soles, but they also produced a collection that used rainforest rubber for their "Soles of the Rainforest" shoes.

Deja shoes from the early 1990s used all recycled material in their construction. The soles were, of course, made from recycled rubber.

Ecosurfaces make many color and texture variations in their range of recycled rubber flooring. Manufactured by Dodge-Regupol, effects include stone, terrazzo, sports flooring, and tiles. Customized colors and motifs produce endless possibilities.

Clothing designers **Gaelyn and Gianfarani** from New York incorporated locally collected discarded bicycle inner tubes in their fall 2002 collection. Working to gain acceptance for the use of recycled rubber in the garment industry, their work applies the rubber in a fashionable manner, sidestepping the eco-friendly "look" frequently seen in other manufacturers. They also use latex sheeting as seen in the copper-colored dress [top left], draping the material like fabric, thus removing it from the fetish arena.

THE CREATIVE USE of discarded materials is a beginning, but we need to think even bigger. The drive to consume non-renewable resources brings high prices and eventually extinction. In his thought-provoking book, *Simple Things Won't Save the Earth*, Robert J. Hunter asks the question: are we even capable of doing what is necessary to save ourselves as a species? Hunter uses the *heve* rubber tree as the book's focal point, presenting it as the "Symbol of our Environmental Dilemma." He compares the gluttonous spectacle of the Space Shuttle's fuel-burning blast-off with the unpretentious 100% natural-rubber landing. His dream of "Rubbertopia" suggests this possible scenario:

1. Petroleum is a non-renewable resource.

2. The world now uses nearly one billion cars and trucks.

3. Even if fuel alternatives become available and widespread, they will still need tires to roll on.

4. Recent estimates say that US oil reserves can last approximately 25-30 years if used solely for the production of synthetic tires. That estimate does not include diesel, gasoline, plastics, and all other petroleum products.

Verdict: Time to develop a 100% natural rubber passenger tire, especially when you consider that natural rubber is superior to the ones we have now. This has been proven by the performance of 100% natural rubber on aircraft and heavy truck tires, yet passenger tires lag behind, averaging five pounds of natural rubber to every seven pounds of synthetic rubber derived from oil.

Although idealistic, it is a logical and worthwhile idea. This passenger-tire revolution could potentially create a sustainable renewable resource to help preserve the rainforests and provide a livelihood for the people who live there.

We use its tears in almost every way never asking, admittedly mystical, questions like why the rubber tree gives up its latex so generously? Even those with latex allergies can turn to another form of rubber plant, which lacks the tropical proteins that cause the allergies: the *guayule* shrub. The Yulex

WHY DOES THE WEEPING WOOD WEEP?

Corporation is working to bring *guayule* latex to a greater market. To build a society that respects the planet and its inhabitants, we must learn to heed the message of rubber, finding worth in less obvious places. Natural rubber is to be celebrated as a modern, eco-friendly material, sustainable, forest-friendly, and fun. Rubber reflects the natural order of organic life and, like our bodies, recycles itself. Erasers perform a twofold disappearing act with each use; in the process of making an image vanish, part of the eraser must disappear as well. The eraser's limited lifetime is not something to be regretted. Tires, shoe soles, pads, and gaskets all illustrate rubber's capacity for perpetually reducing itself through hard work so as not to burden the environment. We would do well to learn by this example. After all, we too only rub up against things until we are gone, leaving just a memory.

A valuable by-product of this "Rubbertopia" would be the cultivation and sale of rubber wood from the trees, which are routinely felled after their productive 25–30 year lives are over. Rubber wood is already used for furniture making in the Far East, and, though the West has been slow to adopt this resource, pressure from consumers concerned about old growth lumber has begun to have an effect on retail outlets. Home Depot stocks rubber-wood parquet flooring, and Plan Toys, pictured here, are made from 100% rubber wood.

BIBLIOGRAPHY

Coates, Austin, *The Commerce in Rubber: The First 250 years*, Singapore & London, 1987; New York, 1989

De Castro, Ferreira, *Jungle: A Tale of the Amazon Rubber Tappers*, London, 1934

Giersch, Ulrich & Ulrich Kubisch, *Gummi: Die Elastische Faszination*, Berlin, 1995

Green, Shirley, *The Curious History of Contraception*, New York, 1971

Hunter, J. Robert, *Simple Things Won't Save the Earth*, Austin Texas, 1997

Katz, Sylvia *Classic Plastics: From Bakelite to High Tech*, London, 1984

Morton, Maurice (ed.), *Rubber Technology*, New York, 1987 (first published 1959)

Rigby, Hugh & Susan Leibtag, *Hardware: The Art of Prevention,* Edmonton Alberta, 1994

Slack, Charles, *Noble Obsession: Charles Goodyear, Thomas Hancock and the race to unlock the greatest industrial secret of the nineteenth century,* New York, 2002

Whittington, E. Michael, *The Sport of Life and Death: The Mesoamerican Ballgame*, London & New York, 2001

Wolf, Howard & Ralph, *Rubber: A Story of Glory and Greed,* New York, 1936

Woshner, Mike, *India-Rubber and Gutta-Percha in the Civil War era*, Alexandria Virginia, 1999

websites

www.balloonhq.com
www.birthcontrol.com
www.bouncing-balls.com
www.by-maze.com
www.cmd.co.uk
www.dalsouple.com
www.decorcraftinc.com
www.droogdesign.nl
www.earthship.org
www.fxsmith.com
www.gaelyn.com
www.lexon-design.com
www.materialconnexion.com
www.monmouthrubber.com
www.olmeca.org
www.propagandaonline.com
www.prostheticskin.com
www.pylones.fr
www.realdoll.com
www.remarkable.co.uk
www.rubber.com
www.rubberplastics.com/the_joy_of_rubber.doc
www.yulex.com

BIOGraPHIeS

Janet Bloor is a graduate of knitwear design from Trent University, Nottingham. She has designed costumes for 25 years, first in London and now in New York, establishing EuroCo Costumes in 1990, and producing costumes for theater, ballet, and movies. She teaches innovative fabric techniques, and her seminars on specialty fabric treatments with silicone rubber take her across the US and Europe.

Henrik Langsdorf is a New York–based graphic designer and illustrator. His illustrations (under the name Otto Steininger) have appeared in *The New York Times*, *The Wall Street Journal*, and other publications in the US, Europe, and Japan.

John D. Sinclair is a freelance writer and editor in Los Angeles whose work appears in various national publications. He is also a filmmaker and screenwriter and has co-directed several award-winning short films.

Gerardo Somoza is a graduate of cinema studies from NYU. He photographs the New York, Paris, and Milan fashion shows, and collections for clients such as Donna Karan and Ellen Tracy. He has disabled twin daughters and specializes in photographing disability related subjects.

ILLUSGraGION CreDITS

Back cover & 2 Courtesy of the artist & Lehmann Maupin Gallery, New York 19 Isolation bearing images: Dynamic Isolation Systems Inc., Ohio 26 Mexican stone ring: South American Pictures; Mayan ball: Christine Mumford 36 Lingerie: Keith Goldstein 38 Sharkskin suit: Mark Weiss; Fabric: Material Connexion® 40 Pen: Sue Broadwell; Bunz jewelry: Jürgen Liedtke 50 & 51 Doormat: courtesy of the artist & Lehmann Maupin Gallery, New York 53 Salt & Pepper: Bianca Tavarez; Think Plant & Pills: Ace Somboon; Soft Urn: courtesy of Jongeriuslab, the Netherlands 54 Frog & duck bottles: Decor Craft Inc., New York/Roni Kabessa 56 Toilet: Arnout Visser, courtesy of Droog Design, the Netherlands; Washtub: courtesy of Jongeriuslab, the Netherlands 57 Squeegie: Peter Rose, courtesy of Cleret; Sink stopper: Propogandist Company, Thailand 58 Switches: Kozo Takayama; Dalí clock: Tomo Futaishi; Straps: courtesy of Droog Design, the Netherlands 60 Calculator: Cooper Hewitt, National Design Museum, Smithsonian Institution, New York, photo: Matt Flynn 62 Smart keyboard: Scogin Mayo 65 Cushions: Mary Ann Weir 66–67 All images courtesy of DNA (Housemarks) Limited and Goodyear Dunlop Tires North America Ltd 71 Flashlights: Decor Craft Inc., New York 78 Tablecloth: Saar Oosterhuis; Plant: Frank Tjepkema, both courtesy of Droog Design, the Netherlands; Jeanne Silverthorne image: courtesy of Mckee Gallery, New York 79 Jil Weinstock images: courtesy of Caren Golden Fine Art, New York, Catharine Clark Gallery, San Francisco, and Frumpkin/Duval Gallery, Los Angeles, photos: Kim Harrington 80 Cheese: Ace Somboon 82 Prosthetic hand: Alatheia Prosthetics, USA; Neck scars: courtesy of Gary Tunnicliffe 83 All images: courtesy of Gordon Smith 84 Costantino image: courtesy of Deitch Projects, New York 85 Realdoll images: courtesy of Abyss Creations 86 Mojo: courtesy of Myla, UK 96 Bags: Craig Morrison, photos: Joel Cockrill; Catsuit: Alexander Brattell & Steven Cook 97 Spikey couch: Peter Ashworth 98 & 99 Courtesy of NASA 102 Earthships: courtesy of Kirsten Jacobsen Earthship Biotecture 103 & 104 Moroccan jug & helicopter: John Bigelow Taylor, thanks to the Museum of International Folk Art.

Acknowledgments

All studio photography is the work of Gerardo Somoza, New York, except as noted in illustration credits

Design and art direction by Henrik Langsdorf, New York

Line drawings by Otto Steininger, New York

Thanks to Pelar Washington, Lisette Rotman, Stephanie Pezulano, Lacey Cope, Austin Trevett, Harris Tweed, and the many friends who saw this project through.

In memory of Eddie and Chico Mendes

First published in 2004 in the United States of America by Thames & Hudson Inc., 500 Fifth Avenue, New York, New York 10110

thamesandhudsonusa.com

Library of Congress Catalog Card Number 2003116698
ISBN 0-500-28490-3

Printed and bound in China by Imago

This RUBBER BOOK belongs to

(My Name) ....

Of the 50,000 articles made of RUBBER I know those recorded on this page.